BEAT ATLAS

A State by State Guide to the
BEAT GENERATION
in America

T0160495

Bill Morgan

Photographs by Allen Ginsberg and Others
Foreword by Nancy J. Peters

City Lights Books • San Francisco

For Jack Hagstrom
A traveler's traveler

Library of Congress Cataloging-in-Publication Data
Morgan, Bill, 1949–
 Beat atlas : a state-by-state guide to the Beat generation in
America / by Bill Morgan.
    p. cm.
 ISBN 978-0-87286-512-9
1. Beat generation—Homes and haunts—United States. 2. Beat
generation—Travel—United States. 3. Literary landmarks—
United States. 4. Authors, American—20th century—Travel.
5. Authors, American—20th century—Homes and haunts. I.
Title.
 PS228.B6M57 2011
 810.9'0054—dc22
                                    2010047784

City Lights Books are published at the City Lights Bookstore,
261 Columbus Avenue, San Francisco, CA 94133.
Visit our website: www.citylights.com

CONTENTS

FOREWORD | Nancy J. Peters

Most people associate the Beat Generation with urban bohemian life in Greenwich Village or in San Francisco's North Beach. Bill Morgan's popular guidebooks—*The Beat Generation in San Francisco* and *The Beat Generation in New York*—offer appealing walking tours of the homes and haunts of Beat writers and their friends in those two key cities. Now, his *Beat Atlas* offers an in-depth review of Beat sites in the rest of the country, the towns the writers came from, and the places they inhabited and celebrated in their work.

The book begins in the Northeast, in Massachusetts, with an extensive survey of literary landmarks in Jack Kerouac's Lowell, the historic mill town where he was born and where he set pivotal autobiographical stories. Browsing through a few random pages, we find New Yorker Gregory Corso in Cambridge, where he was living when his first book, *The Vestal Lady on Brattle,* was published. And then a few pages later, here's Lawrence Ferlinghetti in school at Mount Hermon High, in the hamlet of Gill.

In the Rockies, Morgan leads us through Neal Cassady's down-and-out neighborhoods in Denver, and a later section of the book documents Gary Snyder's early years in the Pacific Northwest.

William Burroughs doesn't immediately come to mind when you think of Midwestern writers, yet he came from St. Louis, Missouri (as did his friends David Kammerer and Lucien Carr, who were to play an incendiary role in the Beat story), and he spent his last sixteen years in Lawrence, Kansas. (In intervening years, he resided briefly in New Orleans and, in the late 1940s, gave marijuana farming in south Texas a try.)

Allen Ginsberg, originally from Paterson, New Jersey, rarely stayed in one place. He traveled incessantly, reading, writing, and promoting poetry wherever he went.

He prodded publishers to issue the work of his friends, and universities to invite them to read. When censors came after them, Allen rose to their defense. When they were broke, he lent or gave them money. A master communicator, Ginsberg spread the literary news and kept poets in touch with one other, generating a culture of connections. Using his enormous energy and talent for publicity as a way to make known the work of the many writers he admired, he capitalized on the idea of a literary "generation" (like the Lost Generation or the Spanish Generation of '27).

The Beats never had a specific agenda for a movement. The writers' subjects and writing styles were distinctly their own, their backgrounds were different, and they had opposing political views. Friendships faded, and lives took new turns. But they all hated the stifling conformist materialism around them and determined to make writing their life.

The term Beat Generation is catchy and the name caught on with the press. But "beat" is an ambiguous word—beaten down? dead beat? beatific? The writers themselves were never consistent in defining it. Such prominent writers as Lawrence Ferlinghetti, Gary Snyder, and even Kerouac and Burroughs distanced themselves from the label "Beat writer," but there can be no doubt that they were part of a sizable postwar generation that propelled American literature and culture in a radical new direction. It seemed an outrageous barbarian invasion to the conservative literary establishment with its traditional publishers of academic, formal poems that had a very small audience. Walt Whitman's democratic spirit had been unloosed in the land, with compelling prose and poetry—spontaneous, audacious, candid, and accessible.

Donald M. Allen's prescient *The New American Poetry 1945–1960* is a good example of the range of this nationwide tide of poetic exuberance. Among the contributors are

Beats Ginsberg, Corso, and Ray Bremser; New York School poets Frank O'Hara, Kenneth Koch, Barbara Guest, and John Ashbery; Black Mountain poets Robert Creeley, Paul Blackburn, Denise Levertov, and John Wieners; and from the San Francisco Renaissance, Lawrence Ferlinghetti, Philip Lamantia, Michael McClure, David Meltzer, Gary Snyder, Philip Whalen, and Lew Welch.

The work of these and other compatible writers began to be widely published in fine letterpress editions of chapbooks and inexpensive paperbacks from adventurous small presses that sprang up from coast to coast. Journals ranged from simple mimeo sheets such as Diane Di Prima and LeRoi Jones's *Floating Bear* to Paul Carroll's breakout *Big Table* to Wally Berman's striking handmade *Semina*, which incorporated drawings, collage, photos, and poems. This countertradition in publishing continues in the zines, mini-presses, online publications, and handmade artists' books that emerge in today's diverse and vibrant literary scene.

Bill Morgan provides a comprehensive bird's-eye view of the proto-Beat presence across America, and this alone illuminates an important area of literary history and geography. But even better, he also maps the complex, ever widening nexus of poets and visionaries who, for half a century, wrote to each other, performed together, supported one another's work, and sustained movement that was dissident, controversial, and ultimately dominant.

PREFACE

"So in America when the sun goes down and I sit on the old broken-down river pier watching the long, long skies over New Jersey and sense all that raw land that rolls in one unbelievable huge bulge over to the West Coast, and all that road going, all the people dreaming in the immensity of it. . . ." Thus begins the beautiful final chapter of *On the Road*. I'll wager that half the people who have read Jack Kerouac's book have also dreamed of going on the road and living the life that Jack described so vividly. Very few of us have ever done it, but, in reading the work of Kerouac, Ginsberg, Ferlinghetti, and other Beat writers, we can share in the experience of what it was like to wander across America in a gentler time.

The Beats were continually on the move, and as a result, important literary events occurred in a variety of locations throughout the country. Too often we feel that we have to visit New York, San Francisco, or Boston to find places where literary history was made. Although these towns are the publishing capitals of America, they aren't the places where most of the Beat writers came from, and they aren't necessarily the places where those writers found their inspiration. Still, I was surprised when I sat down to put this book together that I found "Beat History" in every one of the fifty states. The Beat Generation writers came from everywhere and went everywhere, members of a twentieth-century American literary movement that hailed from all parts of the country. They were born in Massachusetts, Oregon, Kansas, Missouri, New Jersey, and Louisiana. Being so diverse in origin, their writings were not dictated by a single, regional characteristic, so the Beat movement became a national thrust, a joining of like-minded, kindred spirits intent upon exploring the width and breadth of America.

I don't know why it is, but when I read something, I

find myself interested in the biography and background of the author. Where were they from and what experiences did they have? Where were they when they wrote a particular poem or book? I was fascinated to learn that Robert Frost was sitting in his dining room in Shaftsbury, Vermont, on a hot summer morning when he wrote "Stopping by Woods on a Snowy Evening." Zane Grey wrote many of his novels about the Old West in his home in Lackawaxen, Pennsylvania, on the banks of the Delaware River. In contrast to this, I discovered that Kerouac and Ginsberg wrote about places, people, and events as they roamed about the country. They didn't invent as much as record, inspired by what was actually happening around them.

Possibly you jot down your own thoughts in a pocket notebook, collecting people and experiences, just like Kerouac. As you read his work, you'll grow to realize that his books are based on the real people he met on his travels. He shaped their stories into fiction so that his books could flow in an interesting way, sometimes breaking away from a strict adherence to chronology and geography. Artistic license allowed him to change events that took place in Shelton, Nebraska, to Preston, a town on the other side of the state, and he even moved the location of *The Subterraneans* from Greenwich Village to North Beach. Kerouac's remarkable memory and extensive notebooks also made it possible for him to re-create scenes years after they had taken place, and by visiting the actual locations some wonderful discoveries will be made.

It is fun to imagine just what building Dashiell Hammet had in mind when he invented Sam Spade's office, and to wonder whether Melville was looking at the whale-shaped ridge of Mt. Greylock when he wrote *Moby Dick*, but with the Beat writers there is no need to speculate. In *Doctor Sax*, when Kerouac describes the ancient stations of the cross at the grotto, he is describing an actual spot that still exists in modern-day Lowell. The "houseless brown farmland plains rolling heavenward in every direction" that inspired a Ginsberg poem can still be seen in Kansas today. All you need is a map and the desire to get out there and see it yourself. This guide is designed to help footloose souls follow their own interests to some unusual parts of the literary landscape.

Allen Ginsberg vowed to read his masterpiece, "Howl," in every state in the Union at least once, and he managed to achieve that goal before his death in 1997. Maybe these stories of the Beat Generation will inspire another young author to write his own masterpiece and share it with America in the same way. Ginsberg and the others will be with him. Allen said it himself in the last line of "Howl." "I'm with you in Rockland / in my dreams you walk dripping from a sea-journey on the highway across America in tears to the door of my cottage in the Western night."

Organizational Note This is the third book in a series from City Lights. The first two cover the Beat Generation in New York and San Francisco, respectively, and were organized as walking tours to those cities. This volume mentions only a few locations in those two places, but unlike those, this one is not designed to be followed in any predetermined sequence. It is organized first by region and then by state and town within each region. No attempt has been made to put the towns into any order other than alphabetical. Within each section, one location has been selected to highlight a notable place of interest. Lowell, Massachusetts, the birthplace of Jack Kerouac, introduces the book for no other reason than its importance as a Beat site. Other towns within that state follow in alphabetical order. By working with this guidebook in one hand and a trusted map in the other, you can plot your own tour around the country, just like Jack, Neal, and Allen did more than sixty years ago. Grab your rucksack and hit the road!

NORTHEAST REGION

Jack Kerouac, 1953

I. New England States

MASSACHUSETTS

1. Lowell. The mecca for every pilgrim interested in finding the essence of **Jack Kerouac** and his writing is Lowell, Massachusetts. It was in Lowell that Kerouac was born, raised, and eventually buried. It was the quintessential hometown to which Kerouac always longed to return. Thomas Wolfe's words "you can't go home again" were true for Jack, too, although it wasn't for lack of trying. Lowell was the backdrop for many of his books, and strolling its streets is like walking into the pages of Kerouac's novels.

a. Perhaps the best place to begin is at the **Jack Kerouac Commemorative Memorial** in the Eastern Canal Park near the corner of **Bridge and French Streets**. Eight large marble slabs designed by artist Ben Woitena are inscribed with words taken from Kerouac's immortal books. The steles are attractively arranged in a park with trees and benches that provide a meditative place to sit and relax. The memorial was dedicated in 1988 when old friends Allen Ginsberg and Lawrence Ferlinghetti joined Kerouac's widow, Stella Sampas, at the unveiling of the memorial. Lowell continues the tradition of honoring its native son with an annual Lowell Celebrates Kerouac! Festival each October, Jack's favorite month.

Jack Kerouac's birthplace, 9 Lupine Road

b. Jack Kerouac was born in the second floor apartment at **9 Lupine Road** on March 12, 1922, in the Centralville district. His parents, Leo and Gabrielle Kerouac, were first-generation, working-class Canadian-Americans, and the family spoke only French at home. In addition to Jack, the family included his older brother, Gerard, and his sister, Caroline (Nin). A plaque commemorating Kerouac's birth has recently been placed on the house.

c. Kerouac was baptized in **St. Louis de France Church** on **West Sixth Street at Boisvert Street** on March 19, 1922, the same church in which his brother's funeral mass was celebrated only a few years later. Recently the street in front of the church has been named in honor of the Reverend D.W. Boisvert, the priest who christened Jack. In Kerouac's day, before the modern building was constructed, masses in French were celebrated in the basement of the unfinished building.

d. Jack Kerouac's father, Leo, was a printer by trade. In 1923 he opened the **Lowell Spotlite** print shop at **26 Prince Street**. Before long he moved the shop to **463**

Market Street and changed the name to Spotlight Print, and in 1931 he moved it once again to **95 Bridge Street**. As a boy, Jack hung out in his father's shop, and there he learned a good deal about newspapers, sports, and horse racing.

e. Kerouac's father was not a very good businessman, and due to their dire economic problems, the family was forced to move many times. As a result Jack grew accustomed to a transient life, and the migratory nature of his adult years came as no hardship. Most of his early homes still remain scattered around town.

1. In 1925, the family moved to **35 Burnaby Street**. In *Visions of Gerard*, Kerouac places his earliest memories of his brother in that cottage. Jack would have only been three years old when they lived here.

2. Later in 1925, they moved to **34 Beaulieu Street**. It was in this house on June 2, 1926, that Jack's nine-year-old brother Gerard died of rheumatic fever. The tragic nature of his brother's early death played a seminal role in the formation of Kerouac's character, and as an adult Jack memorialized Gerard in several works, including *Visions of Gerard*.

34 Beaulieu Street

3. In August 1927, the family moved to **320 Hildreth Street**.

4. In 1928, they moved to **240 Hildreth Street**.

5. In 1929, they moved to **66 West Street**. There they stayed for three years, their last Centralville address.

6. In 1934, they moved to **16 Phebe Avenue** in the Pawtucketville section of Lowell.

7. Following the devastating flood of the Merrimack

River in 1936, the family moved to **35 Sarah Avenue**.

8. While he was attending high school in 1938, Jack and his family moved to an apartment on the top floor over the Textile Lunch coffee shop at 736 Moody Street. Since then the street has been renamed and the address is now **736 University Avenue**.

9. In 1939, the Kerouacs moved once more, this time to **74 Gershom Avenue**.

10. In the early 1940s, after Kerouac dropped out of Columbia University, he moved back to Lowell where he stayed with his family, who were then living at **125 Crawford Street**.

11. Later in life, following his marriage to Stella Sampas, Jack, Stella, and his mother, Gabrielle, moved back to Lowell and bought a ranch-style house at **271 Sanders Avenue**. Their move came in December 1966, shortly after Gabe had suffered a stroke. The New England winters proved to be too cold for the old woman, and before long they relocated to Florida.

f. While growing up in Lowell, Kerouac attended several local schools. He went to grade school at **St. Louis de France** on **West Sixth Street** next to the church. After that he went to **St. Joseph's School** and graduated from the fifth grade in 1933. He started public school in the fall of 1933 at **Bartlett Jr. High School** at **79 Wannalancit Street**. In 1936 he began classes at **Lowell High School** on **Kirk Street between French and Merrimack Streets**, graduating in June 1939. While in high school he made his mark as a star athlete in track and football. The old clock under which the students hung out in Kerouac's day is still there.

g. The **Merrimack River** features in many of Kerouac's works, especially *Doctor Sax*. In 1936, a major flood of the Merrimack destroyed Leo Kerouac's printing shop and put him out of business. The river can be viewed from many places in town, but Kerouac saw it most often as he crossed the **Moody Street Bridge** (now called the University Avenue Bridge) on his way home from high school. Also featured in *Doctor Sax* is the eerie **Grotto of Our Lady of Lourdes** a mile or so up the Merrimack River behind the Franco-American School at **357 Pawtucket Street**.

Gregory Corso at the Grotto of Our Lady of Lourdes

On a dark, foggy night, this series of fourteen stations of the Way of the Cross made a very strong impression on the young Jack Kerouac. In November 1975, Allen Ginsberg and Bob Dylan came here to film a scene for Dylan's movie *Renaldo and Clara,* and a decade after that, Ginsberg snapped Gregory Corso's picture looking up at this statue of Christ on the cross.

h. The **Lowell City Library**, now named the **Pollard Memorial Library**, at **401 Merrimack Street**, was probably Kerouac's favorite place outside his own home. He spent long hours in the library throughout the 1920s and 1930s, engrossed in every book he discovered there.

i. When Jack Kerouac died in Florida in 1969, his body was flown back to Lowell and a wake was held at the **Archambeault Funeral Home**, still at **309 Pawtucket Street**. Following the wake, the funeral service was held at **Saint Jean de Baptiste Church** on **Merrimack Street**. Four decades earlier Jack had been an altar boy at that church. His old friend, Father "Spike" Morissette, presided over the mass. Edie Kerouac-Parker movingly retold the story of the funeral in her book *You'll Be Okay*.

j. One of the most popular pilgrimage sites for fans of the Beat Generation is **Jack Kerouac's grave** in **Edson Cemetery** on **Gorham Street** in South Lowell. There Kerouac was buried in October 1969, with his family and old friends Allen Ginsberg, John Clellon Holmes, Gregory Corso, Robert Creeley, and Edie Kerouac-Parker in attendance. "He honored life" reads his tombstone. Buried with him is Stella Sampas, his third wife, whom he married in 1966. It was Stella who cared for Jack's mother until Gabrielle's death in 1973. Stella herself died on February 10, 1990. Kerouac is buried in the Sampas family plot next to the grave of his childhood friend, Sebastian Sampas, who died in 1944 during World War II.

Photograph by Helen MacLeod

Lawrence Ferlinghetti visiting Kerouac's grave

k. **Lowell National Historical Park**. The factories of Lowell, which were very much in operation during Kerouac's childhood, later fell on hard times and were closed for many years. Now, some of them have been turned into a museum housing "The Working People Exhibit." In one of the buildings, the Mogan Cultural Center in the **Boott Cotton Mills** at **40 French Street**, is an exhibit that features Jack Kerouac's typewriter and his backpack.

l. After he dropped out of Columbia University in 1941, Kerouac worked as a sportswriter for the *Lowell Sun* on

Kearney Square. Through his father, Jack already knew most of the reporters, and had written articles for the newspaper as a high school student. He stayed for only a few months.

m. By the end of his life, Kerouac had become a hard-drinking alcoholic. In his last years he spent a lot of time at **Nicky's Lounge, 112 Gorham Street**, which was owned by his brother-in-law Nicky Sampas. It remained one of the few places where Jack was always welcome. A decade after Jack's death, Allen Ginsberg brought Bob Dylan here to meet Nicky when they were shooting scenes for Dylan's movie *Renaldo and Clara*.

2. Andover. In the early 1940s **Lucien Carr** attended **Phillips Academy Andover, 180 Main Street**. Later, as a student at Columbia University, it was Carr who introduced the early members of the Beat Generation like Allen Ginsberg, Jack Kerouac, and William Burroughs to one another. Carr was an unruly boy, and his binges with alcohol caused many problems for the Phillips administration. David Kammerer, Carr's scout troop leader from St. Louis, intent on having a sexual liaison with the boy, followed Lucien to Andover from Missouri.

3. Arlington. Robert Creeley was born in Arlington on May 21, 1926. His parents were Dr. Oscar Slade and Genevieve Jules Creeley, and for a while the family lived at **128 Mt. Auburn Street** in nearby Watertown. Robert's father was the head of staff at the **Arlington-Symmes Hospital** on **Hospital Road off Summer Street,** and that

Courtesy of Elsa Dorfman

Robert Creeley

21

is where Creeley was born. That facility is now closed. By the time Bob was four he was living with his mother in her father's house on **Elm Street** in Acton, Massachusetts. In the 1950s Creeley became one of the more important poets associated with Black Mountain College before he moved on to San Francisco and befriended Jack Kerouac and Allen Ginsberg.

4. Boston.

a. Boston has always been the literary capital of New England. None of the prominent Beat writers was born here, although many went to school or lived in the area later. As a boy growing up in Lowell, **Jack Kerouac** visited Boston from time to time. His father took him to see the Red Sox play at **Fenway Park**, and that experience contributed to his lifelong interest in baseball. He even invented his own game of "fantasy baseball" after going to his first major league game.

b. Although poet **John Wieners** was born in nearby Milton, he lived for a good deal of his life in Boston. He attended **Boston College** and graduated in June 1954.

44 Joy Street

That same year, after hearing Charles Olson read his poetry at the **Charles Street Meeting House, 70 Charles Street,** John decided to enroll in Olson's classes at Black Mountain College in North Carolina. In the late 1950s Wieners edited *Measure* magazine, which became a prime outlet for the work of many Beat writers. For the last thirty years of his life, Wieners lived alone at **44 Joy Street** on Beacon Hill. On March 1, 2002, he passed away in **Massachusetts General Hospital** after suffering a stroke. A funeral service was held a week later at **St. Gregory's Church** in Milton, where he was laid to rest in the family plot at the **Milton Cemetery**.

c. Until World War II interrupted his education, Jack Kerouac's best friend, **Sebastian "Sammy" Sampas**, attended **Emerson College** at **120 Boylston Street**. In *Vanity of Duluoz*, Kerouac wrote about his visits to Boston with Sebastian. Sometimes the two young men went to the movies and then sat in the Boston Commons, watching the people pass by. Jack considered going to **Boston College** to play football, but decided instead to attend Columbia. One wonders what his life would have been like if he hadn't made that decision, for it was at Columbia that he met Allen Ginsberg and William Burroughs.

d. In 1942 **Jack Kerouac** signed up for the Merchant Marines at Boston's **National Maritime Union** office on **Scollay Square**, an area that was entirely destroyed by urban renewal. In a letter he described his evenings on the Boston waterfront after waiting all day for a call at the union hall. "I prowl around the docks, 'drinking in the strong cod scent of the wharves,'" he wrote. In *On the Road* Kerouac described a wild night at the **Imperial Cafe** on nearby **Bowdoin Square**. He wound up passed out in the men's room after having downed sixty beers. The Imperial Cafe was one of Kerouac's regular hangouts, and he mentioned it in several other books including *And the Hippos Were Boiled in Their Tanks* and *The Town and the City*.

e. Shortly after **Robert Creeley** married Ann McKinnon in 1946, they stayed in a room at the **Hotel Brunswick** at **520 Boylston Street**.

f. **Allen Ginsberg** was always eager to meet celebrated poets, even if his own poetry owed little to their style. On April 7, 1959, Allen and Peter Orlovsky went to Boston to spend the afternoon with Robert Lowell. The

Allen Ginsberg at the Arlington Street Church

meeting was cordial, although they found that they had very little in common. Lowell often wrote disparagingly about the Beats, but that made no difference to Ginsberg. Over the years Allen read in Boston dozens of times, but one of the most famous readings was in November 1966 at the **Arlington Street Church, 351 Boylston Street**, when Allen delivered a speech titled "Public Solitude" that was more political than poetic. On that occasion he suggested that everyone in America take LSD at least once in their lives. His close friend Elsa Dorfman captured Allen on the pulpit in one of her best photos.

g. The city fathers were not always receptive to the Beat message. In 1963, after Grove Press published William S. Burroughs's *Naked Lunch*, the book was banned in Boston. In January 1965, a celebrated trial was held after bookstore owner **Theodore Mavrikos, 545 Washington Street**, was arrested for selling the book. Even with noted authors testifying in favor of Burroughs's work, the court found that it was obscene, a ruling that was later overturned on appeal. However, the trial and publicity spurred sales of *Naked Lunch* in other parts of the country.

5. Cambridge.

a. **Harvard** is synonymous with the town of Cambridge, just across the Charles River from Boston. As one of the oldest and most distinguished colleges in the country, Harvard has many links with Beat history. The list of Beat generation writers and their contemporaries who attended Harvard is impressive and rivaled only by Columbia in importance. Alan Ansen, John Ashbery, William Burroughs, Gregory Corso, Robert Creeley, Norman Mailer, Frank O'Hara, and Charles Olson all studied at Harvard at one time or another.

b. From 1932 to 1936 **William S. Burroughs** attended Harvard, where he majored in English literature. He attended T.S. Eliot's famous Norton Lectures during his first year, and those talks profoundly influenced his appreciation of modernist poetry. While in college, Burroughs studied the works of Joyce, Kafka, and F. Scott Fitzgerald. During his sophomore year he lived in **Adams House**, where he kept both a pet ferret and a .32 revolver in his room. Then in his junior year he moved to **Claverly Hall on Mount Auburn Street**. Burroughs returned to Harvard again from 1938 to 1940 for graduate studies in anthropology. At that time he lived with his boyhood friend Kells Elvins off campus in a house on a tree-lined street near the Commodore Hotel. Elvins and Burroughs collaborated on a story called "Twilight's Last Gleamings."

c. In 1942, poet **Alan Ansen** graduated from Harvard *summa cum laude*, writing his thesis on Milton's prose. After graduation he continued to study at Harvard for his master's degree. While here, Ansen made friends with two students, Ed Stringham and Alan Harrington, who introduced him to John Clellon Holmes, Allen Ginsberg, and Jack Kerouac. In 1957, Ansen went to Morocco to help Burroughs edit his *Naked Lunch* manuscript. He was to remain in Europe for the rest

Gregory Corso and Alan Ansen

Courtesy of the Alan Ansen Collection

of his life, hosting Beat writers whenever they were in Italy or Greece.

d. **Norman Mailer** began classes at Harvard in 1939 and graduated in 1943. Mailer was a friend of many of the Beat writers, and for a while, after his essay "The White Negro" was published by City Lights in 1960, he was considered to be a writer very much in the Beat tradition.

e. **Robert Creeley** began to take classes at Harvard in 1943. During the mid-forties he dropped in and out of college several times and finally withdrew in July 1947 without graduating. While at Harvard he studied under F.O. Matthiessen, Harry Levin, and Delmore Schwartz. Like Burroughs, Creeley roomed first at **Adams House** and then later at **Lowell House**. Creeley and **Charles Olson,** who also went to Harvard for his Ph.D. but did not graduate, became the closest of friends, and several volumes of their letters to one another have been published by Black Sparrow Press. Creeley is buried in Cambridge in the **Mount Auburn Cemetery**, the final resting place of many famous writers, such as Julia Ward Howe, Henry Wadsworth Longfellow, and Amy Lowell.

f. In 1946, poet **Frank O'Hara** entered Harvard, where his roommate turned out to be artist Edward Gorey. O'Hara published his first poems in the *Harvard Advocate* before he graduated in 1950, eventually publishing his book *Lunch Poems* as one of the City Lights Pocket Poets Series in 1964.

g. **John Ashbery** went to Harvard and received an A.B. *cum laude* in 1949. Ashbery, O'Hara, and Kenneth Koch are commonly thought of as the leading poets of the New York School. This group was closely associated with many Beat writers. Years later when Ashbery retired from teaching at Brooklyn College he recommended that he be succeeded on the faculty by Allen Ginsberg.

h. In 1949, a Harvard Law School graduate named **William Cannastra** moved from Cambridge to New York City to begin his career. He and Jack Kerouac were drinking buddies, and Cannastra's gruesome death in 1950 on a New York City subway became one of the central events in both Kerouac's *Visions of Cody* and John Clellon Holmes's *Go*.

i. One major Beat poet who unofficially went to Harvard was **Gregory Corso**. In 1953, a friend of Corso's, Violette "Bunny" Lang, invited him to live with her in Cambridge. Until 1956 he did just that, sitting in on classes at Harvard and reading books in the Widener Library. During that period he sometimes stayed at **12 Ash Street** in Cambridge. There he wrote a play called "In This Hung Up Age," which was performed by the Harvard Dramatic Workshop (New Theatre Workshop). He also wrote the poems that were published in 1955 by a Cambridge acquaintance, Richard Brukenfeld. This book of poetry

was titled *Vestal Lady on Brattle*, a reference to Brattle Street, one of the main thoroughfares of Cambridge. Corso dedicated the book "For all my friends . . . my beautiful Cambridge friends."

j. **Allen Ginsberg** was never a Harvard student, but he was in residence at **Lowell House** as an invited guest for a while and read in Cambridge on many occasions. In December 1960 he made his first visit to take part in drug experiments conducted by Harvard professor **Timothy Leary**. At the time, Leary had just been appointed director of Harvard's **Center for Personality Research** located at **5 Divinity Avenue**. Tim wanted to experiment with hallucinogenic drugs under controlled conditions so that he could study their effects. After Ginsberg had taken psilocybin and LSD with Leary, the two hatched a plan to turn on the whole country in a less than scientific way, and so the psychedelic revolution was born. On April 30, 1963, Leary was asked to leave Harvard when the college ruled that his scientific method was wanting, but he continued his work independently. In later years Ginsberg returned to Cambridge to perform annually at **Passim's** in **Harvard Square**. He always stayed nearby on **Franklyn Street** at the home of his longtime friend, the photographer **Elsa Dorfman**.

k. During the fifties, the poet **John Wieners** worked for the **Lamont Library** at Harvard. He left his job at the library the day the first issue of his magazine *Measure* arrived from the publisher. Conflicting reports state that it was either a voluntary or an involuntary departure.

6. Greenfield. Herbert Edwin Huncke was born in Greenfield on January 9, 1915. At the time, his parents, Herbert Spencer and Marguerite Bell Huncke, were living at **16 George Street**, an upper-middle-class neighborhood. His father worked nearby for the **Greenfield Tap and**

Die Co. as a manager and salesman. While he was still a baby, Huncke's family moved back to their hometown of Chicago, and it was there that Herbert grew up.

Herbert Huncke's birthplace, 16 George Street

7. Gloucester. As a boy, the poet **Charles Olson** spent his summers in Gloucester. As an adult he made it his home and centered his masterpiece, *Maximus*, here. When Charles was a child, his family rented **Oceanwood**, a cottage in **Barrett's Camp near Stage Fort Park**. Olson displayed early artistic talent and acted in several productions with the **Gloucester School of the Little Theatre** and the **Moorland Players**. By the time he was sixteen, he was working at the **Gorton-Pew Fisheries' processing plant** on the town wharf. Olson's father was a mailman in Worcester, and Charles followed his example by becoming a letter carrier in Gloucester. At six and a half feet tall, he was better known in town for his height than for his poetry, but in 2004, the Charles Olson Society placed a bronze plaque on **28 Fort Square** to commemorate Olson's residence here. It was in this house that Charles wrote *Maximus*.

Many prominent literary figures visited Olson in his Gloucester home over the years. Among them were Donald Allen, Robert Creeley, Diane Di Prima, Michael McClure, and Philip Whalen. In 1966, Allen Ginsberg and Gregory Corso came to pay homage. Ginsberg returned in 1970 to act as pallbearer at Olson's funeral following his death on January 10. He is buried in Gloucester's **Beechbrook Cemetery**.

In April 1977, **Lawrence Ferlinghetti** also visited the Gloucester area and stayed for three weeks in a cabin on

Anasquam inlet. There he wrote his poem "The Sea and Ourselves at Cape Ann."

8. Grafton. Poet **Frank O'Hara** grew up in a white frame house at **16 North Street** in Grafton, a suburb of Worcester. O'Hara was an avid reader and attended **St. Paul's grade school** from 1932 to 1940, directly across **Chatham Street** from St. Paul's Cathedral in downtown Worcester. At the same time he studied music at **St. Gabriel's Music Studio** on the first floor of the St. Joseph's Home for Working Girls and frequently traveled with his parents to hear concerts in Boston. He went on to **St. John's High School** on **Temple Street** in Worcester, from which he graduated in 1944. Immediately upon graduation, O'Hara enlisted in the Navy. In 1952 when O'Hara was twenty-six, he made his last visit to his hometown for the funeral of his Aunt Grace. After that he became estranged from his mother and chose not to return.

9. Holyoke. John Clellon Holmes was born in Holyoke on March 12, 1926. His parents were John McClellan and Elizabeth Franklin Emmons Holmes. His father was a salesman, and the family was forced to move frequently. They lived in six different states during the first few years of John's life. The strain of travel was too much, and his parents divorced, leaving John's mother to raise her two children alone. She was proud of being a direct descendant of Ben Franklin. It's surprising that Holmes, one of the most studious and well-read of the Beats, never finished high school. Instead he dropped out to begin working for the *Reader's Digest*. He is credited with publishing the first Beat novel, *Go*. Holmes was also the first

John Clellon Holmes

person to use the term "The Beat Generation" in print, which he did in a 1952 article in the *New York Times.* He gave proper credit to Jack Kerouac for actually coining the phrase, however.

10. Hyannis. In 1966 **Jack Kerouac** and his mother, Gabrielle, moved to **20 Bristol Avenue**, Hyannis. They had been shuttling back and forth from Florida to the Northeast for several years, never able to settle long in any one place. On September 9, 1966, Gabrielle Kerouac suffered a massive stroke while living in Hyannis. A few weeks later Jack left for a trip to Italy, leaving his mother in the care of Stella Sampas, the sister of his childhood friend, Sebastian Sampas. When he returned, he married Stella in the backyard of this house on November 19 before moving back to Lowell that December. The Bristol Avenue house was also the house in which Kerouac lived when Allen Ginsberg came to visit his old friend. On that occasion the reclusive Kerouac pretended to be his "Uncle Bill" and wouldn't let Allen in. The house numbers have been changed since Kerouac's day, but all the houses on the block are of similar construction and will give you a good idea of his home.

Lowell (see Massachusetts location 1).

11. Newton. In 1960, while he was working as a professor at Harvard, **Timothy Leary** rented a baronial three-story mansion on a hill in Newton Center. To reach the house a visitor had to climb up 185 stone steps from the street. Leary lived in that house with his two children, Susan and Jack, while he ran Harvard's Center for Personality Research. Other experts in the field of drug research, such as Aldous Huxley and Humphrey Osmond, came to the house to confer with him. Allen Ginsberg, Peter Orlovsky, Maynard Ferguson, Charles Olson, and

William S. Burroughs also visited him at his home and took psilocybin under his supervision between the years 1960 and 1962. Ginsberg later said, "Leary had this big beautiful house and everybody there was wandering around like it was some happy cocktail party." In the fall of 1962, Leary moved to a house at **23 Kenwood Avenue** in an attempt to establish a small commune, but the city objected, citing a violation of the single-family dwelling rule. By 1963 Leary was ready to move on to new things, and he let Richard Alpert (later known as Ram Dass) take over the house.

12. Northfield–Mount Hermon. As a young boy, **Lawrence Ferlinghetti** lost his parents and grew up in the care of a well-to-do Bronxville family. They had the means to provide Lawrence with a good education and sent him to a private boy's school at Mount Hermon in 1935. He wrote for the school newspaper, *The Hermonite,* until his graduation in June 1937. His yearbook records his nickname, "Moose," and lists him as Lawrence Furling Monsanto. It wasn't until the fifties, after he had begun publishing his first poetry under the name Ferling, that he restored his family name of Ferlinghetti. Since those days, the boys' school of Mount Hermon has merged with Northfield, the girls' school across the valley, closing one of the campuses in the process.

13. Provincetown. During the 1940s, Provincetown was still an affordable summer destination for bohemian New Yorkers. **Robert Creeley** was probably the first of the future Beats to spend much time there. In 1946–47 he visited Provincetown with friends and moved there shortly after his marriage to Ann McKinnon in 1946.

The whole group of "subterraneans" that clustered around the San Remo cafe in New York City also spent their summers in Provincetown. Among them were Bill

Cannastra, Alan Ansen, Joan Haverty (later to become the second Mrs. Kerouac), and Helen Parker. Allen Ginsberg met Parker and experienced his first, albeit brief, sexual relationship with a woman. At one time she had been engaged to John Dos Passos, and she knew Hemingway in Cuba, so she became Allen's link with a more established literary community.

In the 1970s, **Gregory Corso** lived with various friends at **199 Commercial Street** and **14 Center Street**. He often received his mail at the church at **236 Commercial Street**. Provincetown also became **Norman Mailer**'s home during the final years of his life.

14. Springfield. Psychedelic drug advocate **Timothy Francis Leary** was born in Springfield on October 22, 1920. At the time of his birth, his father, Timothy Leary Sr., was serving as a captain at West Point Military Academy.

Timothy Leary

Leary's mother, Abigail Ferris Leary, and the baby were living in an apartment at **43 Magazine Street** when his father returned to set up a dental office at **292 Worthington Street**. When Tim was thirteen, his alcoholic father abandoned the family. Still, Leary managed to get a good education, and in 1938 he graduated from **Classical High School**, the best public school in the city. Although he was only an average student, he was accepted at **Holy Cross College** with the help of a friendly priest.

15. Swampscott. Poet **Larry Eigner** was born in a hospital in nearby Lynn on August 7, 1927, but his family's home was in Swampscott. Eigner, a victim of cerebral palsy, spent his entire life in a wheelchair. Because of his physical condition, his parents believed that he would never be able to communicate with them, but he taught himself to use the typewriter as a teenager. Then, in 1949, he heard Cid Corman reading poetry on the radio and it impressed him so much that he began to write poetry himself. His work was strongly influenced by Charles Olson and the Black Mountain group, and he became a close friend of Robert Creeley. Eigner lived in Swampscott with his parents until 1978, when he moved to Berkeley, California, to live with his brother. Eigner died in Berkeley on February 3, 1996.

16. West Acton. When **Robert Creeley's** father died, he and his mother moved to **Willow Street** in West Acton. At age 10 he entered the **West Acton Grammar School**, where he excelled as a student.

17. Worcester.

a. Although strongly identified with Gloucester, **Charles Olson** was actually born in Worcester on December 27, 1910. He was the only child of Karl and Mary Hines Olson, who lived at **16 Mitchell Street** with Mary's father. As he grew up the family also lived at **4 Norman Avenue**. From 1917 to 1924, Olson attended the **Abbott Street Grammar School** before going on to **Classical High School**, where he graduated with honors in 1928 as president of his class. Although Olson went away to college, he returned briefly to teach at nearby **Clark University** during the 1930s.

Charles Olson

Courtesy of the Allen Ginsberg Trust

b. Abbie Hoffman was born in Worcester on November 30, 1936. His parents, John and Florence Schanberg Hoffman, owned the **Worcester Medical Supply Company**. The family had an apartment at **264 Chandler Street**, which was then in the center of Worcester's Jewish neighborhood, before moving on to a larger apartment at **5 Geneva Street** and a house at **6 Ruth Street**. Abbie attended **Seaver Prep** and **Classical** high schools, the best public schools in the city. Rebellious by nature, Abbie was once suspended for punching a teacher. As a result, in September 1953, he transferred to **Worcester Academy** and graduated in 1955. Leaving Worcester he enrolled in **Brandeis University** in Waltham, Massachusetts, intending to become a doctor.

After Hoffman's first wife became pregnant, he left graduate school at the University of California, Berkeley, and returned to Worcester, where he was appointed staff psychologist in the admissions office of **Worcester State Hospital**. In the mid-1960s, Hoffman and his wife, Anita, became political activists and moved to New York City, where they befriended Allen Ginsberg and helped to form the Youth International Party, commonly known as the Yippies. Abbie came to national prominence as one of the Chicago Seven, the collective name given to the defendants who were tried for disrupting the 1968 Democratic National Convention. Ginsberg testified for the defense in their 1969 conspiracy trial. In his later years, Hoffman won the respect of his hometown and received the key to the city from the mayor of Worcester. When he died in 1989, over 900 people attended his memorial service and marched from his boyhood home to the synagogue.

c. Timothy Leary attended **Holy Cross College** at **1 College Street** from 1938 until 1940 and lived in room 38 on the fourth floor of **Fenwick Hall**. A mediocre student, he spent much of his time playing poker and taking bets on sporting events before transferring to West Point. In 1993, Leary returned to Holy Cross to give a lecture titled "How to Use Your Brain."

MAINE

1. Brunswick. For a short period of time **Lucien Carr** was a student at **Bowdoin College**. Here and elsewhere, Carr found himself being stalked by an older admirer from St. Louis, David Kammerer. For more details, see the Andover, Massachusetts, entry.

2. Northeast Harbor. While **Robert Creeley** was a student at Harvard in the mid-1940s he visited his mother here on holidays. At the time she lived in a new house on **Summit Road**.

3. Old Orchard Beach. In November 1961, **Jack Kerouac** visited Old Orchard Beach for the purpose of finding land on which he could build a little cabin in the woods. By then, the ravages of fame and alcoholism had taken their toll, and he was eager to retreat from everything and everybody. He never quite found a place to settle down, even though he dreamed of living here "among the Canucks," as he put it.

4. Orono. The **University of Maine at Orono** has been the host for many literary conferences and symposiums, several under the auspices of the National Poetry Foundation. These were attended by many Beat writers including Helen Adam, Amiri Baraka, Robert Creeley, Allen Ginsberg, Joanne Kyger, and John Wieners. In the eighties, while at one of these conferences, Ginsberg visited the great photographer Berenice Abbott, who

Allen Ginsberg and Berenice Abbott

maintained a summer home in nearby Monson. Allen, who was learning about the art of photography himself, appreciated her advice on the subject. "Don't be a shutterbug," she warned him when he began taking multiple pictures of her.

NEW HAMPSHIRE

1. Chichester. In 1932 one of the lesser-known poets associated with the Beat Generation, **Edward Marshall**, was born, the son of Chichester farmers Harry and Lena Marshall, who lived on Bear Hill. Marshall's autobiographical statement in Don Allen's *The New American Poetry 1945–1960* notes that he received the "basic 3 R's in Concord, NH, then University of New Hampshire and New England College, Henniker, NH." Allen Ginsberg admired one of Marshall's poems, "Leave the Word Alone," and used it as a model for his own master-piece, "Kaddish."

Lawrence Ferlinghetti and Richard Eberhart at Dartmouth

2. Hanover. Dartmouth College is located in Hanover and, like all major universities, it has hosted many Beat readings and lectures over the past fifty years. The **Dartmouth College Library** houses letters between Allen Ginsberg and Richard Eberhart, the well-known poet and critic who taught at Dartmouth for thirty years. One of the letters that Ginsberg wrote to Eberhart on May 18, 1956, detailed his method of composition for his landmark poem "Howl." Ginsberg was afraid that Eberhart would miss the importance of the structure of his poem, as so many other literary critics had, so he laid it all out in one long letter. Instead of ignoring the brash, egotistical poet, Eberhart was receptive to his ideas, and they became friends.

3. Littleton. In the late 1940s, **Robert Creeley**, his wife Ann McKinnon, and their baby Lina moved to **Rock Pool Farm** about six miles outside of Littleton off the main road to Lisbon, New Hampshire. They had geese, chickens, rabbits, and a goat, but little else in the way of creature comforts. Creeley was not a dedicated farmer and devoted more time to poetry than to farming. Friends like Denise Levertov came to visit him here from time to time. Then, in 1949, Ann and Bob's second child died two days after his birth in the old farmhouse. In January 1951, after falling behind on their mortgage payments, the Creeleys moved to a cheaper place in nearby Raymond.

4. Nashua. Jack Kerouac's parents, **Leo and Gabrielle Levesque Kerouac**, were both from Nashua, a town just across the state line to the north of Lowell. Gabrielle worked in a shoe factory in Nashua, an occupation she relied upon throughout her life. They were married on October 15, 1915 at **St. Louis de Gonzague Church, 48 W. Hollis Street**.

Most of the Kerouac family is buried in Nashua with the exception of Jack. In 1926, Jack's older brother Gerard was the first of his immediate family to be buried in the family plot in the **St. Louis de Gonzague Cemetery** at **752 W. Hollis Street**. Gerard was followed in death by Leo in 1946 and Gabrielle in 1973. In 1996, the last Kerouac, Jan, the daughter that Jack never acknowledged, was laid to rest in the same plot.

5. Plymouth. Even though **Robert Creeley** was a bright student, he had to take a battery of tests to get into the prestigious **Holderness School** at **33 Chapel Lane**, just outside Plymouth. In 1940, with his sister's help, he won a scholarship to the school, at the time under the leadership of headmaster, Reverend Edric Weld. Creeley published his first stories in the school paper, *The Holderness Dial.* In 1943, he graduated from Holderness and went on to study at Harvard.

VERMONT

1. Barnet. The **Tail of the Tiger** in Barnet was the first meditation center that the Buddhist spiritual leader Chögyam Trungpa founded in America. It is located just

Peter Orlovsky and Peter Hale at Karma Chöling

off **West Barnet Road** at **369 Patneaude Lane** and has since been renamed **Karma Chöling**. Both Allen Ginsberg and Peter Orlovsky became students of Trungpa during the early 1970s and visited this retreat center numerous times. They also invited friends to come with them, and even non-Buddhist William S. Burroughs stayed for a two-week retreat in the summer of 1975. Trungpa instructed Burroughs to leave his typewriter at home and to do no writing while he was here, but Burroughs openly admitted that he was more interested in writing than he was in any sort of spiritual enlightenment. He brought a notebook with him and wrote *The Retreat Diaries,* which he published the following year. Trungpa died in Halifax in 1987 and his body was brought to Karma Chöling for cremation in the meadow on May 28. Ginsberg attended and wrote the poem "On Cremation of Chögyam Trungpa, Vidyadhara" for that occasion. In 2010 Peter Orlovsky's funeral ceremony was held in the meditation hall here.

2. Bennington. **Bennington College** on **Route 67A** has long been considered one of the best liberal arts colleges in the country. **Carolyn Robinson** (later **Cassady**) took undergraduate classes at Bennington with Martha Graham, Erich Fromm, Ted Roethke and other celebrated teachers during the early forties. She graduated with the class of 1944, earning a bachelor's degree in drama and then moved to Denver to continue her education. There, her life took an unexpected turn when she met Neal Cassady and Jack Kerouac. Neal wrote to Jack upon meeting her, "There's only one thing wrong with her—too middle class—Ha! Bennington. Oh well." Neal and Carolyn married in 1948 and raised three children together.

Carolyn Cassady

Twenty years later, in 1964, poet **Anne Waldman** graduated from Bennington College. Anne, like Carolyn, was also interested in drama, but she used her theatrical training to electrify her poetry performances in the years that followed.

3. Calais. Every year, poet, playwright, and publisher **Kenward Elmslie** spent his summers in Calais at a house he named "Poet's Corner." Elmslie's partner, the artist **Joe Brainard**, maintained a studio on the property until his death in 1994. Over the years Elmslie's Z Press published work by many noted poets like John Ashbery, Ron Padgett, Joe Brainard, and James Schuyler. Kenward's own work often combines poetry with art, music, and theater.

4. Putney. During his high school years, composer **David Amram** attended the experimental **Putney**

41

School at **418 Houghton Brook Road**. The boarding school had been founded in 1935 by Carmelita Hinton, a pioneer in progressive education. This was all long before Amram supplied the jazz accompaniment for readings by Jack Kerouac, Philip Lamantia, and Howard Hart in the 1950s.

5. St. Albans. Poet **Paul Blackburn** was born in St. Albans on November 24, 1926, to parents William Gordon and Frances Frost Blackburn. Frances was a poet and children's author herself. In 1930 the family was living on a farm along Orchard Road in South Burlington, and it was during that year that Frances and William divorced. Paul's mother left the young boy and his sister in the care of his grandparents and resumed her career as a writer in New York. When Blackburn was fourteen, his mother took him to live with her in Greenwich Village. There he was exposed to writers and artists and, with his mother's encouragement, began to write poetry.

6. St. Johnsbury. In 1950, while **Robert Creeley** was living in nearby Littleton, New Hampshire, he hosted

a weekly radio program of prose and poetry on a St. Johnsbury station. The program required a lot of work and wasn't very popular, so it lasted only a few weeks. Nearly fifty years later, following the death of Allen Ginsberg in 1997, Allen's lifelong partner, **Peter Orlovsky**, bought a small frame house at **44 Green Street** in St. Johnsbury, in order to live close to the

Peter Orlovsky on the porch at 44 Green Street

Photograph by Gordon Ball

Buddhist community at Karma Chöling. This was still his home when he passed away from lung cancer in 2010.

RHODE ISLAND

1. Newport. In March 1943, **Jack Kerouac** enlisted in the Navy and was sent to the **Newport Naval Base** for basic training as an apprentice seaman. He worked on his novel *The Sea Is My Brother* during off-hours, but the regimentation of military life did not suit him. After a few weeks of training, during which time Kerouac repeatedly refused to obey orders, he was sent to the base hospital for a psychological evaluation and then transferred to the naval hospital in Bethesda, Maryland, for further examination. On June 30, 1943, he received what the Navy called an "indifferent discharge" and was given $50.67 travel money to return home.

2. Providence.

a. Second-generation New York School poet **Ted Berrigan** was born in Providence on November 15, 1934, as Edmund Joseph Michael Berrigan Jr., son of Edmund and Margaret Dugan Berrigan. His Irish Catholic father worked at **Ward's Baking Company** in Providence, and Ted went to various local schools in their blue-collar neighborhood of South Providence. Berrigan's later poem "Things to Do in Providence" gives an idea of Ted's feelings about his hometown. "Crash / Take Valium Sleep / Dream &, forget it. . . . "

Ted Berrigan with Pat Mitchell in Providence

Following graduation from high school, Berrigan went to **Providence College**, where he stayed only one year, earning poor grades. During the Korean War he spent three years in the army before going back to school at the University of Tulsa under the G.I. Bill.

b. Like Ted Berrigan, **Clark Coolidge** grew up in Providence. Clark was born here on February 26, 1939. After graduating from **Classical High School** in 1956, Coolidge went on to **Brown University**, where he majored in geology. He left school in 1958 to travel around the country. Coolidge became associated with the language poets around New York before moving to the West Coast in 1967 to join Beat poet David Meltzer's band, Serpent Power.

c. **Robert Creeley** joined the faculty of **Brown University** in 2003, where he taught as Distinguished Professor of English until his death in 2005. The **Hay Library** at Brown houses one of the most comprehensive literature collections in the country and has large holdings of Beat Generation writing. In 1964 the Hay was the first university library to host an exhibit devoted exclusively to the work of the Beats.

CONNECTICUT

1. Hartford.

a. Usually **Jack Kerouac** lived with other people, but he did have his own apartment, only once, during the fall of 1941, and that was at **106 Webster Street**. That summer Jack's father had landed a job in West Haven and Jack stayed there with his parents, but in the autumn he decided to strike out on his own. The room he found here was $4.50 a week with a cooking stove. While in Hartford he wrote a collection of stories that he called *Atop an Underwood*. During the same period, Kerouac used the return address of **1 Warner Street**, a block away from his address on Webster, but it is not clear whether he moved to another apartment or was having someone else receive mail for him, which was often his habit. In the local **Hartford Public Library**, Kerouac read books by Wolfe, Saroyan, Halper, Dos Passos, and William James.

b. Poet **Helen Adam** was born in Glasgow, Scotland, in 1909 and came to visit Hartford in 1939 to attend a cousin's wedding. Instead of returning, she settled in town with her sister, Pat, and mother, Isabella. Ten years later they all moved to New York City.

2. Manchester. While living in Hartford during the fall of 1941, **Jack Kerouac** pumped gas at the **Atlantic Whiteflash station** in Manchester. Jack rode to and from work with Bob, someone whom at least one biographer compared to Neal Cassady.

3. Middletown.

a. On March 30, 1988, at the age of sixty-two, **John Clellon Holmes**, the author of *Go,* died in the hospice unit of the **Middlesex Memorial Hospital** on **Main Street**. He lived much of his life in nearby Old Saybrook. It was Holmes who used the term The Beat Generation for the first time in print, in *The New York Times* on November 16, 1952.

b. **Charles Olson** attended **Wesleyan University** on **Washington Street** from 1928 through 1933. After graduation, he continued on at Wesleyan for his M.A. degree and wrote his thesis on "Growth of Herman Melville, Prose Writer and Poetic Thinker." Olson's first book, *Call Me Ishmael* (1947), grew out of that work.

4. New Haven. On November 24, 1958, **Allen Ginsberg** gave his first reading at **Yale** and was surprised by the large turnout. The reading had originally been scheduled for a small seminar room in **Phelps Hall**, but when nearly 300 people showed up, it had to be moved to the larger **Harkness Hall**. Ginsberg returned to Yale on May 1, 1970, during the student strike here. In addition to Allen, French author **Jean Genet** gave a speech that was reprinted immediately by City Lights. During the strike, students were tear-gassed and Ginsberg chanted "omm" to calm the crowd, just as he had in Chicago two years earlier.

5. Norfolk. **James Laughlin**, the owner and publisher of New Directions Books, had a home in Norfolk for much of his life. New Directions actually began in 1936 in a little cottage on the grounds of Laughlin's Aunt Leila's house in Norfolk while he was still a college student. **Kenneth and Miriam Patchen** lived in that same stone cottage in 1939 as Laughlin's guests. Later Jay and his wife lived in a house at **305 Mountain Road** less than a mile from the village center. Laughlin was the heir to the Jones and Laughlin steel fortune, and at Ezra Pound's suggestion he decided to use his inheritance to publish some of the greatest works of contemporary literature. He specialized in publishing work that other commercial houses were afraid to touch, especially translations of foreign writers. In addition to Hesse, Lorca, and Sartre, he also published the works of Gregory Corso, Robert Creeley, Lawrence Ferlinghetti, Denise Levertov, Michael McClure, Ezra Pound, Gary Snyder, William Carlos Williams, and a host of others. Laughlin died of a stroke on November 12, 1997, at the age of 83, as he was being rushed to a hospital in Sharon.

6. Old Saybrook. In 1952, with the generous advance **John Clellon Holmes** received for the paperback rights to his novel *Go,* he helped his mother buy an old Victorian house at **11 Shepard Street**. Then in 1956 he and his second wife, Shirley Allen Holmes, moved into a small school house next door at **15 Shepard Street**, which they renovated themselves. There he worked on books like his jazz novel, *The Horn.*

15 Shepard Street

Jack Kerouac visited him several times and liked the area so much that, during a September 9–15, 1962, visit, he shopped unsuccessfully for a house of his own. When he left, he drunkenly asked the cab driver to take him to Lowell (125 miles away) at great expense. Holmes wrote an essay about Jack's visits and his alcoholism, later published as *Visitor: Jack Kerouac in Old Saybrook.* John and Shirley lived together on Shepard Street until they passed away in 1988 within a few weeks of one another.

7. Storrs. The **University of Connecticut**'s main campus at Storrs has a distinguished library that houses several important collections of Beat Generation materials. In the **Thomas J. Dodd Research Center** are portions of the archives of poets Ed Sanders and Diane Di Prima, as well as letters and manuscripts by Bill Berkson, Ted Berrigan, Robert Creeley, Fielding Dawson, Ed Dorn, Frank O'Hara, Philip Whalen, and John Wieners. **Ann Charters**, one of the first scholars to study the writings of Jack Kerouac and the author of his first biography, has taught at the university for many years. She was born nearby in Bridgeport, Connecticut, in 1936.

8. Uncasville. In 1961 **Ed Sanders** and a group of pacifists attempted to board the newly commissioned

Courtesy of the Allen Ginsberg Trust

Ed Sanders

submarine **USS *Ethan Allen*** in the Connecticut River near here. The sub was one of the first to be armed with Polaris missiles. Sanders was arrested as a "witness for peace" and sent to the **Montville State Jail** in Uncasville. Kept there August 8–24, 1961, Sanders wrote his "Poem from Jail" on the backs of cigarette packs and smuggled them out in his shoes. The poem was published by City Lights in 1963 as his first book.

9. West Haven. In 1941, while **Jack Kerouac** was attending Columbia University, his parents moved from Lowell to the Bradley Point area of West Haven in pursuit of work. They lived in a little cottage that once stood at **5 Bradley Point** in Seabluff facing out onto Long Island Sound. Jack spent the summer of 1941 with them before moving on to his own apartment in Hartford. Later, their cottage was razed and the area was converted into a park.

Allen Ginsberg

II. Middle Atlantic States

NEW JERSEY

1. Paterson. What Lowell was to Jack Kerouac, Paterson was to **Allen Ginsberg**. When he was four, Ginsberg's family moved from Newark to Paterson to be closer to the school where his father taught. In addition to being an English teacher, **Louis Ginsberg** was well-respected as a local poet. Due to economic hardship brought on by the ever-increasing expenses of Allen's mother's

Courtesy of the Allen Ginsberg Trust

Allen Ginsberg, Newark, 1926

hospitalizations, Ginsberg's family moved many times during his youth.

a. Homes

1. The first Ginsberg home in Paterson was an apartment at **83 Fair Street**, where they lived from 1930 to 1933. After nearly ten years of commuting to Paterson from Newark, Louis Ginsberg was happy to be close to his job, but Allen remembered it as a "sad rooming house on dingy Fair Street."

2. By 1933, Ginsberg's mother, Naomi, needed psychological treatment, and Louis did the best he could to keep her in private sanitariums. To economize they moved to a house on **Carbon Street**, which they shared with the Field family.

3. A few months later, in 1934, Louis found an affordable white frame house with a small yard at **155 Haledon Avenue**, where the family remained until 1936. During the day, Louis taught school, but in the evenings when he had a spare moment he sat at his small wooden desk and wrote poetry.

4. The Great Depression weighed heavily on the Ginsberg family. In 1936 the school district cut teacher salaries and once again the family had to find cheaper quarters. They rented a second floor apartment down the hill at **72 Haledon Avenue**, where they stayed until 1939. In 1937, while they were living here, Louis's book of poems, *The Everlasting Minute,* was published by Liveright Publishing Co. Instead of bringing in extra money, the publication was subsidized by Louis to the tune of $2,000. All the unsold copies of the book were stored in the

apartment. These were to be some of his mother Naomi's darkest days and were candidly described by Ginsberg in *Kaddish*.

5. From 1939 until 1942, the family stayed in an apartment building at **288 Graham Avenue** on the east side of town. While living here Allen did volunteer work for the local Democratic Party.

6. In 1943 the family moved once more, this time to **324 Hamilton Avenue**. They lived here during the summer of the year Ginsberg graduated from high school and enrolled in Columbia University.

b. Schools. Ginsberg attended several different schools as a result of his family's frequent moves. In 1931, he entered first grade at **P.S. 1**. By 1939, when he graduated from the sixth grade, he was attending **P.S. 6**. That fall he began classes at **Central High School**, the same school where his father taught. Then, two years later, he was transferred to **Eastside High School** until his graduation in June 1943.

Allen Ginsberg, high school yearbook

c. During high school, Ginsberg worked part time at the **Paterson Public Library** at **250 Broadway**. There he shelved books for twenty cents an hour.

d. In order to earn money for college, Ginsberg tried his hand at factory work. One job that he kept for only two weeks was in a ribbon factory near **River Street**. He was fired because he couldn't master manual labor, but the experience occasioned his 1950 poem "How Come He Got Canned at the Ribbon Factory." That same year, during the Christmas holiday, Ginsberg worked at the **Paterson Post Office**.

Courtesy of the Allen Ginsberg Trust

Allen Ginsberg at the Great Falls

e. In Ginsberg's day Paterson was an industrial town, but it is also the location of a spectacular natural wonder. The Great Falls of the Passaic River slice right through the middle of the city. **Allen Ginsberg** and **William Carlos Williams** visited the falls together on several occasions and the falls figure prominently in Williams's epic book-length poem *Paterson*. Williams even quoted from Ginsberg's letters in some of the later parts of his poem. It was Williams who gave Ginsberg the idea of mining his journals for prose nuggets that could be converted into poetry.

f. On the night of July 8, 1976, eighty-year-old **Louis**

Ginsberg died quietly in his home at **48A Elmwood Terrace, Elmwood Park**, with his second wife Edith at his side. Allen visited him often during his final days and wrote a series of poems titled "Don't Grow Old," which deal with his father's failing health. As he flew back to his father's funeral, Allen penned his most moving song, "Father Death Blues."

2. Asbury Park. Edie Kerouac-Parker, Jack Kerouac's first wife, spent many of her summers at the seaside in Asbury Park both before and after her 1944 marriage to Jack. Her wealthy grandmother maintained a summer house at **312 Sixth Avenue** here. In her memoir, Edie said that once when Kerouac visited her at this address, she dressed him up with seashells and earrings and "passed him off as a gypsy."

3. Bayonne. On their first trip to the East Coast, in December 1946, **Neal Cassady** and his young bride, **LuAnne Henderson**, rented a room in Bayonne at **Mrs. Cohen's Rooming House**, then at **91 West 46th Street**. Their romantic idyll didn't last long. Within a month the couple split up and LuAnne took a bus back to her mother's house in Denver.

4. Belmar. Not far from Asbury Park, Belmar is another popular summer resort along the Jersey shore. **Allen Ginsberg** spent many of his summer vacations with his father's family in Belmar while his mother was away in mental hospitals. During the 1930s Louis Ginsberg's brothers and sisters rented a house on **16th Avenue**.

5. Bordentown. Ray Bremser lived in Bordentown from 1952 until 1958, but it wasn't by choice. Ray had been sentenced to do time in the **Bordentown Reformatory** for two counts of armed robbery. In prison he educated himself and read everything he could find in the prison library. He also began a correspondence with Allen Ginsberg and Gregory Corso. Before long Bremser began to write poetry himself, and LeRoi Jones published some of it in early issues of *Yugen* magazine. Upon his release he met Jones and became part of the New York City jazz and poetry scene.

6. Camden. Many Beat writers have visited Camden in order to pay homage to the memory of one of America's greatest poets, **Walt Whitman**. In 1959, Allen Ginsberg visited Whitman's house at **328-330 Mickle Boulevard** for the first time. He wept when he saw Whitman's old gray hat and eyeglass case resting near the poet's bed. The famous lilac bush in the backyard was nearly dead, but to Ginsberg it didn't tarnish the joy of his pilgrimage. Today the house in which Whitman passed away in 1892 is a museum. Whitman also designed his own tomb, which can be found nearby in the **Harleigh Cemetery** at **1640 Haddon Avenue**.

7. Jersey City. Poet **Ray Bremser** was born in Jersey City on February 22, 1934. He was the son of Gertrude and

Frank Bremser, a bandleader and pianist who sometimes worked at the Palace Theater in New York. For a while the family lived at **243 South Street**. However, little is known about Bremser's early childhood. He grew up in New Jersey and enlisted in the military at age seventeen, but soon went AWOL and was discharged. For a few months, he worked in an

Ray Bremser

Courtesy of the Allen Ginsberg Trust

incandescent lightbulb factory in Jersey City, which is mentioned in his book, *Poems of Madness*.

8. Lyndhurst. William Carlos Williams was buried in **Hillside Cemetery** at **742 Rutherford Avenue** following his death on March 4, 1963. That year he was posthumously awarded the Pulitzer Prize for poetry for his book *Pictures from Brueghel*.

9. Montclair. In his cousin's Montclair dental office, **Allen Ginsberg** had his first high on laughing gas (i.e., nitrous oxide). As he sat on a park bench in front of the doctor's office, Ginsberg wrote down his immediate impressions. A "Trackless Transit Corporation" bus drove past and everything began to make wonderfully ironic sense to him. His long poem "Laughing Gas" came out of this experience. Right away he recommended gas to his father. "This drug seems to automatically produce a mystical experience. It's a very safe drug you ought to contact someone at Rutgers who's doing experiments with it and try it—like a comic movie," he wrote.

10. Morris Plains. During the 1930s and 1940s, **Naomi Ginsberg**, Allen Ginsberg's mother, was treated in Greystone Hospital (now called Greystone Park Psychiatric Hospital) on **West Hanover Avenue** for severe schizophrenia. After her death Ginsberg wrote his greatest poem, *Kaddish*, in her memory. In it he tells of the mental illness that brought her to places like Greystone.

Allen and Naomi Ginsberg

11. New Brunswick.

a. Rutgers University is located in downtown New Brunswick, and it was from here that Allen Ginsberg's father graduated in 1918. With his degree, **Louis Ginsberg** became an English teacher in the Paterson school system for the next forty years, devoting his spare time to raising his family and writing poetry, a means of expression that both his sons adopted. As a result of Louis's example, Allen always thought of poetry as "the family business."

b. In 1940 **Jack Kerouac** played for the Columbia football team in a game at the newly built **Rutgers Stadium**, which was replaced in 1994. Kerouac was still a freshman and the Rutgers game was one of only two games that Jack participated in that year. In *Vanity of Duluoz* Kerouac remembered the day mainly because he wasn't sent in until late in the fourth quarter. Columbia lost 18-7, but Jack showed a good running attack for the brief period he was on the field. The earliest existing postcard written by Jack Kerouac was sent from New Brunswick to his friend Sebastian Sampas on the day of that game.

12. Newark.

a. Allen Ginsberg was born in Newark's **Beth Israel Hospital, 210 Lyons Avenue**, at two o'clock in the morning on June 3, 1926. He was named Irwin Allen by his parents, Louis and Naomi Ginsberg, but they always called him Allen. The Ginsbergs were living in an apartment at **163 Quitman Street** at the time with their first son, Eugene, who celebrated his fifth birthday the day before Allen was born. When Allen was four, the family moved to Paterson.

Following his death on April 5, 1997, Ginsberg was cremated and a portion of his ashes was interred beside the grave of his father in the **Gomel Chesed Cemetery**,

McClellan Street and Mt. Olivet Avenue, near the Newark Airport. On Allen's headstone are lines from his poem "Father Death Blues." "Father death once more farewell / Birth you gave was no thing ill / My heart is still as time will tell."

b. LeRoi Jones was born in Newark on October 7, 1934, as Everett LeRoi Jones. His parents were Coyette (Colt) LeRoy and Anna Lois Russ Jones. Jones first went to **Central Avenue School** and later to **Barringer High School**, from which he graduated in 1951. Coincidentally, Barringer was the high school that both of Allen Ginsberg's parents, Louis and Naomi, attended thirty-five years earlier. In 1951–52, Jones attended the **Newark campus of Rutgers University** on a scholarship. After that he enrolled in Howard University in Washington, but he did not graduate.

Amiri Baraka (aka LeRoi Jones)

In 1966, when LeRoi Jones left his wife (writer Hettie Jones) and two daughters, he returned to Newark and became a prominent black activist. He established a black cultural center in a slum building and called it **Spirit House**. In Newark he married Sylvia Robinson (later called Amina) and had five more children with her. During the Newark riots, a period of racial unrest in 1967, Jones was arrested by the police and beaten. He was sentenced to two and a half years in jail for the alleged possession of a weapon, but was later acquitted. In 1968 he assumed the name Ameer Baraka, a name that was given to him by the orthodox Muslim leader Heshaam Jaaber. Later he was awarded the title Imamu by Maulana Ron Karenga. Since 1974, when he dropped that title from his name, he has been known as Amiri Baraka. He has lived in Newark for many years on **South 10th Street**.

c. **Neal Cassady** married his third wife, model **Diana Hansen**, in Newark's **City Hall** at **920 Broad Street** on July 10, 1950. Their witnesses were Allen Ginsberg, John Clellon Holmes, and Alan Harrington. Two hours after the wedding ceremony, Cassady was back on the road heading to San Francisco, where his second wife, Carolyn, was waiting for him. For a while he tried unsuccessfully to juggle families on both coasts.

Paterson (see New Jersey location 1).

13. Rutherford. Although **William Carlos Williams** is most often associated with Paterson, since *Paterson* is the title of his epic four-volume work, he was actually born and made his home in nearby Rutherford. In January 1957, when Allen Ginsberg, Jack Kerouac, Gregory Corso, and Peter Orlovsky visited the old doctor, he was living with Flossie, his wife, in a house at **9 Ridge Road**. Williams was supportive of Ginsberg's poetry and wrote an introduction for Allen's first book, *Howl and Other Poems*. Williams died in Rutherford in 1963.

14. Union City. On February 5, 1942, **Janine Pommy** (later **Vega**) was born in Union City. She grew up in a typical working-class family. Her father was a milkman. At school she was a good student and graduated as the class valedictorian. As a teenager in the 1950s she liked to go to Greenwich Village and began to sit in on poetry readings at the local coffeehouses. She met Herbert Huncke, Elise Cowen, and Allen Ginsberg and fell in love with Allen's companion, Peter Orlovsky, on these visits. Everyone encouraged her to write, and in 1968 City Lights published her *Poems to Fernando* in its Pocket Poets Series.

NEW YORK

1. Albany. In the fall of 1950 **Jack Kerouac** met **Joan Haverty** in New York City and impetuously married her a few weeks later. Almost immediately she became pregnant, making Kerouac doubt his paternity, even though all later evidence proved that the child was his. In need of financial support, Joan returned to her mother's house upstate to have her baby. On February 16, 1952, she gave birth to **Jan Kerouac** in an Albany hospital. Jan followed in her father's footsteps and became a writer.

2. Bear Mountain. Jack Kerouac's days on the road had an inauspicious beginning at Bear Mountain. On July 17, 1947, he left New York City determined to hitchhike straight across Route 6, all the way from the Hudson River near Bear Mountain to Ely, Nevada. It took him all day just to get from Manhattan to the Bear Mountain Bridge, where he noted, "Route 6 arched in from New England." Then, just as he was dropped off at the traffic circle where **Routes 6 and 9W** intersect, it began to rain in torrents. He ran a quarter mile to stand under the roof of what he called an "abandoned English style filling station," until finally someone stopped and gave him a ride back to Newburgh. Discouraged, he aborted his hitchhiking plans and returned to New York City. From there he took a bus as far as Chicago.

3. Bearsville. Albert Grossman, Bob Dylan's manager, founded the **Bearsville Studios** at **Wittenberg Road and Route 212** in 1971. Since that time many well-known albums have been recorded in this studio. The Rolling Stones even rehearsed at the studio for their

Courtesy of the Allen Ginsberg Trust

Andy Clausen

1979 American tour. Tiny Bearsville is also the home of poet **Andy Clausen** who lived here with **Janine Pommy Vega** until her death in December 2010.

4. Big Wolf Lake. North of Tupper Lake, high in the Adirondack Mountains, is Big Wolf Lake. During the Depression, **Lawrence Ferlinghetti** spent his summer vacations at his foster family's lodge on this lake. Their chauffeur, Gerhard Rulof, taught Lawrence how to fish, but later drowned in a fishing accident.

5. Brentwood. Brentwood, Long Island, was once the home of **Pilgrim State Hospital**, but the massive buildings are now abandoned. The mental hospital, which was named after Dr. Charles W. Pilgrim, opened in 1941. One of the patients on the 2,000-acre Pilgrim State campus was **Naomi Ginsberg**, Allen's mother. She was given a prefrontal lobotomy here on November 14, 1947, from which she never fully recovered. Between 1946 and 1959 as many as two thousand lobotomies were performed by doctors at Pilgrim State. Naomi died here on June 9, 1956, and was buried in a nearby cemetery the following day. **Carl Solomon**, the friend to whom Allen Ginsberg addressed "Howl," received shock treatments here in the 1950s and 1960s.

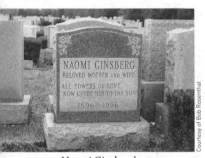

Naomi Ginsberg's grave

6. Buffalo. The history of the Beat Generation in Buffalo is centered around the **University of Buffalo, or SUNY Buffalo**, as it came to be known.

a. Robert Creeley taught at SUNY Buffalo for nearly

forty years beginning in the mid-1960s. By 1967 he had become a tenured professor; he was made the Gray Professor of Poetry and Letters in 1978 and the Samuel P. Capen Professor of Poetry and Humanities in 1989. In the 1980s he lived at **12 Mayfair Lane**, and in later years he, his wife Penny, and their children lived at **64 Amherst Street**.

b. One of the factors that originally brought Creeley to Buffalo was the presence of **Charles Olson**, who taught at SUNY from 1963 until 1965. When Olson was appointed Visiting Professor of English, he rented a place in nearby Wyoming, New York, and taught courses on "Modern Poetry" and "Myth and Literature." One of Olson's students at Buffalo was Harvey Brown, who established the Frontier Press and published work by Olson and his followers.

c. The presence of Charles Olson was also a determining factor for **John Wieners**, who came to study at SUNY Buffalo for two years beginning in 1965. Wieners earned his master's degree under Olson's tutelage and stayed on as a teaching fellow. His book *Pressed Wafer* was published in 1967 by the Upstairs Gallery Press in Buffalo.

d. In late 1964, when **Gregory Corso** and his first wife, Sally November, separated, he left her in Cleveland and came to Buffalo looking for work. He began teaching a course on his literary hero, Percy Bysshe Shelley, at SUNY in January 1965, but was fired when he refused to sign the "Feinberg Certificate," a document the state required as a condition for employment. It asked all applicants to swear that they were not members of the Communist Party, and although Gregory was by no means a communist, he chose to protest the un-American nature of the oath. It was one of the few times that Corso took a political stand on anything. During this period, he engaged in the use of heroin and his health suffered as a result. While in Buffalo Corso lived with friends at **117 Highland Avenue**.

e. Corso also lived from time to time with **Allen DeLoach** at **805 West Ferry Street**. DeLoach was the publisher of *Intrepid*, a mimeo magazine that featured the work of many Black Mountain and Beat poets during the 1960s and 1970s. DeLoach was also the editor of a widely-read anthology, *The East Side Scene*.

f. Another member of the SUNY Buffalo faculty was author **Leslie Fiedler**. Fiedler was a respected literary critic and editor, and his essays were often at odds with the "new criticism" popular at the time. In 1967, Fiedler was arrested in Buffalo on trumped-up drug charges after someone planted a small amount of marijuana in his house. As a result he lost his job with the college, but he remained in Buffalo until his death on January 29, 2003, living for a time at **194 Morris Avenue.**

g. The **University Library** houses one of the truly great collections of poetry in America. From 1979 to 2007, librarian Robert Bertholf collected widely in the field, and as a result the library contains major collections of Helen Adam, Ed Dorn, Robert Duncan, Charles Olson, Jonathan Williams, William Carlos Williams, and many other important poets.

7. Canton. In 1999, **Diane Di Prima** received an honorary Doctor of Literature degree from St. Lawrence University at **23 Romoda Drive**. Di Prima read at the school several times, including one reading in 1973 that was recorded for John Giorno's influential Dial-A-Poet series.

8. Cherry Valley. In 1968 **Allen Ginsberg** bought the eighty-acre **East Hill Farm** a few miles east of the tiny village of Cherry Valley on Route 50. Calling it a farm was an exaggeration, but Ginsberg wanted a place where his friends could escape from the stress of city life. He

Allen Ginsberg and Gregory Corso in the front yard of the Cherry Valley farmhouse

hoped that Kerouac, Corso, and Huncke would use the peaceful rural location as a retreat, but Kerouac died the following year without ever visiting the farm. In fact Ginsberg and Corso were at the farm when they received the news of Jack's death. Gregory went into the woods and carved Kerouac's name on a tree in the name of American poetry. Although the farm attempted to be self-sufficient, it could never pay for itself. There was no electricity or running water and the growing season was very short. In spite of the hardships, nearly all Ginsberg's friends visited the farm during the late sixties and early seventies. After Ginsberg left the farm, he let other poets live there. Anne Waldman, Ray and Bonnie Bremser, and Charles and Pam Plymell all lived in Cherry Valley. Here the Plymells founded Cherry Valley Editions and published not only Ginsberg's work, but also the writing of Herbert Huncke and some of the other visitors to the farm.

9. Cooperstown. The French translators and publishers of many Beat authors, **Mary Beach** and **Claude Pelieu**, lived at **85 Chestnut Street** for many years. In 1987 they invited painter, filmmaker, and musicologist **Harry Smith**, who was indigent, to live with them. He proved to be a demanding house guest. Smith, a close friend of Allen Ginsberg, had compiled the influential *Anthology of American Folk Music* recordings four decades earlier. Pelieu died in December 2002 after he and Mary had moved to **50 Henry Street** in nearby **Norwich, New York**, and in 2006, Beach passed away at the age of 86.

10. Cortland. On September 13, 1971, poet and translator **Paul Blackburn** died of esophageal cancer while living in Cortland. He had taught at SUNY Cortland for several years before he passed away at the age of forty-five.

11. Dannemora. The **Clinton Correctional Facility** was the maximum-security prison where **Gregory Corso** was imprisoned from 1947 to 1950. As a teenager, Corso was repeatedly in trouble with the law, and when he turned eighteen he was sent to jail for theft. He spent his years at Dannemora reading voraciously in the prison library. When he was released in 1950 he was determined to become a poet, and within a few months had met Allen Ginsberg and other members of the emerging Beat Generation.

12. Delmar. **Joan Haverty**, Jack Kerouac's second wife, was born in the Jamaica Hospital in Queens but grew up with her family at **7 Bothwick Avenue** in Delmar, a town close to Albany. On November 17, 1950, Haverty married Jack Kerouac in New York City, and the newlyweds visited her mother in Delmar for the Thanksgiving holiday. When Joan became pregnant, Kerouac abandoned her and the baby and she returned here to live with her mother. All this is related in her memoir, *Nobody's Wife*.

13. Elmira. **Lucien Carr**, a close friend of Kerouac,

Ginsberg, and Burroughs, spent two years in the **Elmira Reformatory** for the manslaughter of David Kammerer. The judge sentenced him to an indefinite term, which began on October 9, 1944. A model prisoner, Carr was released two years later and returned to New York City, where he found a job with United Press, retiring forty-seven years later. He maintained his silence about the killing to the end of his life.

14. Fire Island. Poet **Frank O'Hara** was struck and killed by a dune buggy on July 25, 1966, as he walked along Fire Island beach late at night. He was only forty years old at the time of the freak accident. When Allen Ginsberg learned of his friend's death he wrote the poem "City Midnight Junk Strains" in his memory.

15. Geneva. When **Herbert Huncke** was a boy of twelve, he was unhappy living in Chicago with his family. He ran away from home several times and once got as far as Geneva before the police picked him up. They took him to the local station and called his father to come pick him up. Huncke wrote about his early life in *The Herbert Huncke Reader*.

16. The Hamptons. Following his death in 1966, **Frank O'Hara** was buried in the **Green River Cemetery** on **Accabonac Road** in East Hampton, locally known as Springs. He had spent several happy summers in the Hamptons with his close friends Fairfield Porter, Larry Rivers, James Schuyler, and Willem DeKooning. On his small tombstone is the line "Grace to be born and live as variously as possible."

17. Huntington. **Walt Whitman** was born in Huntington on May 31, 1819. His home has been preserved as a historic site and is now open to the public at **246 Old Walt**

Whitman Road in West Hills. It houses a wide range of Whitman artifacts, including some original manuscripts. Whitman's work had a major influence on Allen Ginsberg and others in the Beat Generation. Allen's most popular poem, "A Supermarket in California," described an imaginary meeting with Walt Whitman in a modern-day grocery store.

18. Loudonville. Joan Vollmer was born in 1924 and raised in Loudonville, a suburb of Albany. While her father, David W. Vollmer, managed a factory that produced photographic film, the family lived in a large brick house at **21 North Loudon Heights**, just off Route 9. As a child, Joan attended the **St. Agnes School** in Albany. In 1942 she left to attend Barnard College in New York City, where she made friends with Edie Parker. Through Edie she met Jack Kerouac, Allen Ginsberg, and William S. Burroughs, who later became her common-law husband.

Joan Vollmer

Courtesy of the Allen Ginsberg Trust

In September 1951, Joan's life ended tragically when Burroughs accidentally shot her in the forehead during a drunken game of William Tell.

19. Millbrook. In the fall of 1963, the fabulously wealthy Hitchcock family, heirs to the Mellon banking fortune, invited **Timothy Leary** and **Dick Alpert** to conduct psychedelic research on their 2,500-acre estate at the edge of town. Leary had recently been let go from Harvard and needed someplace to continue his experiments. Some of the estate's buildings were converted into sleeping quarters and meditation rooms for Leary and his many guests. In 1964 Ken Kesey and the Merry Pranksters visited Millbrook in their psychedelically painted school bus, which they had christened "Further." It was driven by Kesey's new best friend, Neal Cassady, and even Allen Ginsberg was onboard for a short leg of the journey. They received a cool reception from Leary. He did not want attention drawn to the estate, and the Merry Pranksters always managed to attract a lot of attention. The following year Diane Di Prima moved to the estate with her husband, Alan Marlowe. Leary hosted many visitors, from Maynard Ferguson and R.D. Laing to Charles Mingus. Mingus, in fact, once accidentally locked himself in the mansion's giant walk-in refrigerator. Leary's days at Millbrook came to an end in 1966 when the 64-room mansion was raided by G. Gordon Liddy, then a local sheriff, years before Liddy went on to become one of Richard Nixon's Watergate "plumbers."

On December 12, 1964, Timothy Leary married Nena Von Schlebrugge at the **Grace Chapel Episcopal Church** in Millbrook. Nena was a beautiful blonde fashion model

Courtesy of the Allen Ginsberg Trust

Ken Kesey (third from right) and friends on the porch of Timothy Leary's Millbrook estate

who had appeared on the covers of *Vogue*, *Mademoiselle* and *Harper's Bazaar*. Poet Gregory Corso had introduced Leary to Nena. After her brief marriage to Leary, she married the Buddhist scholar Robert Thurman, with whom she had a daughter, actress Uma Thurman.

20. New York City. Manhattan. The city contains some of the most important sites related to the Beat Generation. For details about those sites, please refer to *The Beat Generation in New York*. As a frame of reference, five key points of interest are listed below.

a. Columbia University, **Broadway and West 116th Street**.

b. Ginsberg's apartment, where he wrote *Kaddish*, **170 E. Second Street**.

c. Kerouac's apartment, where he wrote *On the Road*, **454 W. 20th Street**.

d. William S. Burroughs's apartment, **69 Bedford Street**.

e. Gregory Corso's birthplace, **190 Bleecker Street**.

In that guide, not much attention was paid to the outer boroughs, which are covered in greater detail below.

21. New York. The Bronx.

a. **Carl Solomon** was born on March 30, 1928, and raised in the Bronx in a number of apartments, including one at **581 Timpson Place** in 1930. His father, Morris H. Solomon, sold smoked fish and was successful enough to employ a live-in Irish maid named Bridget Daley. Allen Ginsberg met Solomon during a stay at a mental hospital in the late 1940s and dedicated his most famous poem, "Howl" (originally titled "Howl for Carl Solomon"), to him. Throughout his life Solomon lived in many apartments in the Bronx. In 1968 he lived at **3120 Wilkinson Avenue** in apartment 3J, and by 1992 he was living at **3147 Sands Place**. For most of his life

Carl Solomon, fishing at City Island in the Bronx

Carl either lived with his mother, Anne Solomon, or was a patient in various mental hospitals.

b. **Jack Kerouac** received a scholarship to **Horace Mann High School** at **231 West 246th Street** for the school year 1939–1940. He lived with his mother's stepmother in Brooklyn and took the subway two hours each way to the Bronx campus. At Horace Mann he made friends with **Henri Cru**, who was depicted as Remi Boncoeur in Kerouac's novels. Later Jack returned to the Bronx in two different capacities. In 1944, he was incarcerated in the **Bronx County Jail** as a material witness in the murder case of David Kammerer. Then in 1951, he returned as a patient at the **Kingsbridge VA Hospital, 130 W. Kingsbridge Road,** where he stayed for two months while he was treated for a severe case of phlebitis.

c. Poet **Jack Micheline** was born in the Bronx on November 6, 1929, and lived at **1156 Colgate Avenue**. He was named Harold Martin Silver by his parents, Herman and Helen Micheline Silver. Later in life he adopted his mother's maden name as his own. Micheline's first book of poems, *River of Red Wine,* was praised by both Jack Kerouac and Dorothy Parker.

d. Poet **Harold Norse** was born in the Bronx at **Lincoln Hospital, 234 East 149th Street,** on July 6, 1916. Because his mother was unwed, Norse referred to himself as a "Bastard Angel" and gave that name to his publications. After begging his mother for information about his father, Harold learned only that he had been a piano player in a silent movie theater.

e. Artist **Larry Rivers** was born in the Bronx on August 17, 1923, and named Irving Grossberg. He changed his name in 1940 when his band was introduced in a New York City bar as "Larry Rivers and the Mudcats." Before becoming a painter, he had planned to be a saxophone player.

f. Poet **Jack Hirschman** was born in the Bronx on December 13, 1933. He was the son of Stephen Dannemark and Nellie Keller Hirschman. As a teenager Hirschman attended **Dewitt Clinton High** and graduated in 1951. His family lived at **1138 Wheeler Avenue** and then moved across the street to **1125 Wheeler** before they relocated to **Morris Avenue**. Between 1951 and 1955 Hirschman worked his way through Long Island University and City College as a copy boy for the Associated Press and married Ruth Epstein before graduating with his bachelor's degree in English Literature.

22. New York. Brooklyn.

a. Poet **Alan Joseph Ansen** was born in Brooklyn on January 23, 1922, to William and Bessie Blum Ansen.

He grew up in Woodmere, Long Island, went to Harvard, and became W.H. Auden's secretary, Burroughs's editor, and a close friend to Ginsberg and Corso.

Courtesy of the Allen Ginsberg Trust

Alan Ansen in front of his home in Woodmere, Long Island

b. **Hubert Selby Jr.** was born in Brooklyn on July 23, 1928, and raised in the Bay Ridge section. His father came from Hungary and worked as a superintendent for a building in Manhattan at **258 Riverside Drive**, and for several years they lived in the super's apartment in that building. Selby's most famous book, *Last Exit to Brooklyn,* is sometimes referred to as an example of Beat literature, portraying as it does the grittier side of urban life. In 1959 Selby lived at **626 Clinton Street** in the shadow of the Brooklyn Battery Tunnel. A bar stands on Clinton Street today, named Last Exit in his honor.

c. **Diane Di Prima** was born in Brooklyn on August 6, 1934, to Francis and Emma Mallozzi Di Prima. It was a difficult birth and her mother nearly died. At first she and her mother recuperated with her grandparents in the Bronx, but before long they moved back in with her large Italian-American family on **First Place** in Brooklyn. At the age of seven, Diane began to write poetry, and at the age of thirteen she transferred to Hunter High School in Manhattan.

d. During World War II **Allen Ginsberg** trained with the U.S. Maritime Service, and in April 1945 he worked as a spot welder for the Eastern Gas and Fuel Association in the **Brooklyn Navy Yard** with the title "helper shipfitter." Ginsberg was not suited for manual

Allen Ginsberg (second row from top, third from left) with his class at Sheepshead Bay, 1945

labor, and the job lasted only a month. At the end of that summer he underwent more training at the **Sheepshead Bay Station** of the Maritime Service, this time learning the duties of a ship's steward. **William S. Burroughs** went to the same station in August 1945, but with the end of the war in sight, his services were no longer needed and he stayed at the Sheepshead Bay base for only a few days.

e. Poet, artist, and musician **Tuli Kupferberg** was a graduate of **Brooklyn College** at **2900 Bedford Avenue**. He went on to become a founding member of The Fugs, a sixties satirical rock band. **Harold Norse** was also a Brooklyn College alumnus graduating with the class of 1938. In 1979 **Allen Ginsberg** filled in for poet John Ashbery, who was on temporary leave from his teaching position here. Ginsberg did such a good job that he was asked to fill Ashbery's chair as a full professor when John retired. During the years Ginsberg taught at Brooklyn, the Wolfe Institute helped him host an important series of readings that brought nearly every member of the Beat Generation to campus. At the time of his death in 1997, Ginsberg had just decided to retire from teaching.

f. Jack Kerouac lived with his mother's stepmother in her apartment at **293 State Street** while he attended classes at Horace Mann High School in the Bronx. He commuted two hours every day to reach the school. After classes were over he had to spend several hours at football practice, so he had very little spare time and did most of his homework on the subway.

23. New York. Queens.

a. Born in Brooklyn on July 16, 1934, **Hettie Cohen** (later **Hettie Jones**) moved with her family to **139-36 228th Street** in Laurelton at the edge of Queens in 1942. She attended **P.S. 156** and later commuted to **Far Rockaway High School** until she left for college in 1951. Eventually she left her traditional Jewish family for life in Greenwich Village, where she met, married, and had two children with poet LeRoi Jones, now known as Amiri Baraka. Together they published *Yugen* magazine and Totem Press books. Hettie Jones eventually became a writer herself, producing a marvelous memoir about the period titled *How I Became Hettie Jones.*

b. Although she was born at the Manhattan Women's Hospital on West 110th Street on September 27, 1935, **Joyce Glassman** (later **Johnson**) spent her first few years growing up in Kew Gardens, Queens, and Bay Ridge, Brooklyn. While she was still quite young the family moved to 620 West 116th Street in Manhattan, and that is the apartment she remembers most vividly as a girl. Her recollections of being a woman during the heyday of the Beat Generation are revelatory and appropriately titled *Minor Characters*, because the group of Kerouac, Ginsberg, Burroughs, et al., was definitely a boys' club, with the women playing minor roles.

c. In 1943, **Jack Kerouac**'s parents moved to **133-01**

Crossbay Boulevard, Ozone Park. In this apartment Kerouac wrote his first novel, *The Town and the City*. After his father Leo died here of cancer in 1946, Jack and his mother stayed on for two more years. Recently the city has placed a plaque on the building to commemorate Kerouac's residence.

d. From Ozone Park, **Jack Kerouac** and his mother Gabrielle moved to an apartment at **94-21 134th Street** in the Richmond Hill section. While living here, Jack wrote *The Subterraneans, Maggie Cassidy,* and *Doctor Sax* on a typewriter at the kitchen table. When Kerouac married Joan Haverty in 1950, the couple stayed here for a few weeks in December, but Joan soon discovered that there was no room for her in the close relationship between Jack and his mother. After the couple divorced, Joan sent the police to this apartment to charge Jack with failure to pay child support for his daughter, Jan Kerouac.

e. On April 21, 1949, **Allen Ginsberg** was a passenger in a car that was chased down by police in Bayside, Queens. Allen's friends **Herbert Huncke, Little Jack Melody,** and **Vickie Russell**, had been using his apartment to store stolen goods, and even the car they were riding in was hot. When Little Jack missed his exit off **Francis Lewis Boulevard to Northern Boulevard**, he turned down a one-way street the wrong way, right in front of a cop. A chase ensued, the car rolled over, and everyone was arrested and charged with grand larceny. To avoid jail, Ginsberg was sent to a mental hospital, and it was there that he met Carl Solomon, to whom he would address "Howl."

24. North Tarrytown. On July 10, 1950, Neal Cassady married **Diana Hansen**, who lived at **190 Courtland Street** in North Tarrytown. By then she was pregnant with Neal's baby and Neal "did the right thing" by marrying her. He proposed that he should live with her in New York for six months of the year and then live with his other wife, Carolyn, in California for six months. Diana had been looking for work as a fashion model and kept an apartment in Manhattan at **319 East 75th Street**, but when the baby, Curtis Neal Hansen, was born on November 7, 1950, she moved back upstate to be closer to her mother.

25. Northport.

a. Jack Kerouac moved to Northport to escape the pressure that fame had imposed on him in New York City. In the spring of 1958, with the help of his friends Robert Frank and Joyce Johnson, Jack located a house at **34 Gilbert Street** and moved in with his mother and their cats. Gabrielle wanted to escape the cold winters by moving to Orlando, Florida, so after shipping all their furniture, Jack stayed behind in the empty house and tried to find a buyer.

b. In October 1959, after **Jack Kerouac** sold the Gilbert Street house, he decided not to move to Florida as he had planned. He bought another house in Northport at **49 Earl Avenue**, a small cottage surrounded by a white picket fence on a tree-lined street. Jack converted the attic into a writing studio with a small table and a simple straight back chair. While the Kerouacs were living in this house, Jack's favorite cat died and his mother buried it in the backyard. Jack returned to this house in November 1959 with Lew Welch and Albert Saijo after their *Trip Trap* trek across the country from California.

c. In November 1962, after a short stay in Florida, **Jack Kerouac** moved back to Northport once more and bought a house at **7 Judy Ann Court** just off Dogwood Road. His mother arrived on December 24, 1962, and they stayed there until August 1964. This is the house where Kerouac was living when Neal Cassady, his new girlfriend Anne Murphy, and a tennis player from Stanford named Bradley Hodgman, visited in the summer of 1963. While in Northport, Jack spent a good deal of time drinking with the painter Stanley Twardowicz, who had a studio conveniently located above a liquor store on Main Street. Together they often frequented local bars like **Gunther's** and **Murphy's**.

d. **Peter Orlovsky**'s mother, sister, and brothers also lived in Northport from time to time. The Orlovskys were very poor, and at one point they all lived in a converted chicken coop. In 1964, Peter's mother Kate Orlovsky moved to the top floor of an apartment building at **155 Main Street**.

26. Ossining. In the 1950s, **Herbert Huncke** spent time in **Sing Sing Correctional Facility**. He was frequently in jail. Huncke calculated that during his lifetime he spent a total of eleven years behind bars.

27. Plainview. Allen Ginsberg's only brother, **Eugene Brooks**, lived at **986 Old Country Road** for most of his adult life. He dropped the family name Ginsberg when he became a lawyer in the 1940s, thinking it would be better for business not to sound "too Jewish." Like his famous brother and father, Eugene was also an accomplished poet, and in 1973 he published his own book of poems, *Rites of Passage*. Allen frequently brought his "Beat" friends along to meet Eugene, who often helped them with legal matters.

28. Putnam Valley. Musician **David Amram** lives on a small farm just off the Taconic Parkway on **Peekskill Hollow Road**. Until he lost his New York City apartment in 1996, David had the best of both worlds, a country farmhouse and a city loft. When a fire destroyed many of his possessions in 1999, he rebuilt the house and continued his nonstop schedule of composing, writing, and performing, while still finding time to mow the fields and prune the apple trees.

29. Rochester. Poet **David Meltzer** was born in Rochester on February 17, 1937. His parents were Louis and Rosemunde Lovelace Meltzer. Even though Meltzer spent all of his adult life in California, his roots were in this area.

30. Schenectady. William Cannastra was one of two sons born to upper-middle-class immigrant parents from Italy. He grew up on **Pennsylvania Avenue**, a once tree-lined street near the Mount Pleasant ball fields. In high school, Cannastra met a local girl, Joan Haverty (later the second Mrs. Kerouac), who was from nearby Delmar, and in 1949 they both moved to New York City. There they met a lively crowd with whom they partied endlessly. Jack Kerouac dubbed the group "the subterraneans." Cannastra's life ended abruptly on October 12, 1950, when he was killed in an accident. Drunk, he tried to climb through a subway car window as it pulled out of a station and he was dragged to his death on the tracks. This tragedy became the central event in John Clellon Holmes's novel *Go*, as well as an important part of Kerouac's *Visions of Cody*.

31. Utica. Poet **Ray Bremser** spent most of his years after 1978 in Utica. There he was finally able to break some of his addictions before he died of lung cancer in the **Faxton Hospital, 1676 Sunset Avenue**, on November 3, 1998. His ashes were scattered on Allen Ginsberg's farm near Cherry Valley.

32. West Point. It may be surprising to learn that the LSD guru **Timothy Leary** was a cadet at the U.S. Military

Academy at West Point in 1940. It will not be a surprise to learn that he was demerited out the following year after breaking the cadet conduct code repeatedly. He completed his education in Alabama, before entering Harvard to start the research that eventually led to the psychedelic revolution.

33. Woodmere, Long Island. Born in Brooklyn, **Alan Ansen** grew up in Woodmere. As a boy, he attended the exclusive **Woodmere Academy** at **336 Woodmere Boulevard**, took violin lessons, and collected books. In 1938 Ansen entered Harvard, where he would graduate with honors. On October 13, 1937, he was shocked to learn that his mother had died on the S.S. *Queen Elizabeth* as she returned from Europe. Sadly, his father passed away a few months later on March 18, 1938. This story may sound familiar to anyone who has read William Gaddis's book *The Recognitions*, and indeed Gaddis and Ansen were close friends. After graduating from college, Ansen lived with a refined elderly aunt at **816 Bryant Street** in Woodmere. In *On the Road* Kerouac described the unpleasant arguments between Ansen and his aunt and even suggested that Ansen was just waiting for her to die so that he could inherit her house. In 1954, when she passed away, he rented the house to Gaddis and left for Europe, where he played a major role in the editing of Burroughs's book *Naked Lunch*. Ansen never returned to live in the United States and died in Athens on November 12, 2006.

34. Woodstock.

a. Woodstock's most famous resident was **Bob Dylan**, who lived here in the late sixties. His home was in the art colony of **Byrdcliff**, a few miles out of town. Dylan lived here in 1966 when he was injured in a motorcycle accident that dramatically changed his life and his music. Although there are several versions of the story, it seems that he was driving along **Zena Road south of Highway 212** on his Triumph 500 when he ran off the road at a sharp turn near a barn known as the Old Zena Mill. Many friends visited him while he was convalescing in Woodstock, including Allen Ginsberg.

b. Musician, publisher, and poet **Ed Sanders** has also lived in Woodstock since the 1960s. He and his wife Miriam are deeply involved in local politics and ecological movements. For years he was the publisher of the *Woodstock Journal*, the local newspaper, and he covered environmental issues while somehow managing to write poetry, publish books, tour with his rock group, The Fugs, and raise a daughter.

Ed Sanders in his yard at Woodstock

c. As a child, **Allen Ginsberg** spent several summers with his family at **Indian Point Camp** near Woodstock. He experienced some of his happiest moments here, before his mother's mental illness took complete control of her.

35. Yonkers.

a. On March 24, 1919, **Lawrence Ferlinghetti** was born at **106 Saratoga Avenue** in South Yonkers, the youngest child of Charles and Clemence Albertine Mendes-Monsanto Ferling. Lawrence's father, born in Brescia, Italy, anglicized his name to Ferling in the 1930s, and Lawrence restored the family name in 1955. Just before Lawrence was born his father died, causing Lawrence's mother to have a nervous breakdown for which she was hospitalized. Baby Lawrence was raised by an aunt in

France and did not know his mother or brothers until later in life.

b. In 1925, **Lawrence Ferlinghetti**'s aunt, Emily Monsanto, took a job as governess for the daughter of Presley and Anna Lawrence Bisland, who lived at **Plashbourne**, a mansion at **51 Carlton Road** in Lawrence Park West. Aunt Emily was caring for young Lawrence at the time, so the Bislands allowed her to bring the boy with her to live in the third-floor servants' quarters. One day Emily disappeared forever, leaving Lawrence behind. The Bislands never legally adopted Lawrence, but cared for him and sent him to the **Riverdale Country School at 5250 Fieldston Road** in the Bronx where he boarded during the school year. From 1928 through 1934 he lived with Zilla Larned Wilson in downtown Bronxville and attended public school.

c. **Joel Oppenheimer** was born at **303 Hawthorne Avenue** in Yonkers on February 18, 1930, and was raised there by his parents, Leopold and Kate Rosenwasser Oppenheimer, proprietors of a leather goods store. Joel went to Cornell University for a year before enrolling in Black Mountain College, where he studied under Charles Olson and Paul Goodman. In New York City he was instrumental in organizing the poetry readings that developed into the St. Mark's Poetry Project. Oppenheimer died of lung cancer in Henniker, New Hampshire, on October 11, 1988.

PENNSYLVANIA

1. Feasterville. In 1937, when composer **David Amram** was six years old, his family moved from Philadelphia to a farm in Bucks County. There they had 160 acres on the **Bustleton Pike** just north of the Summerton Springs swimming pool. The stone house where David learned to play piano has survived, but the farm was broken up by developers long ago and the barns and outbuildings were razed.

Also in this part of Pennsylvania was the small apartment on **Sugan Road** in **Solebury Township** near New Hope where activist and Yippie **Abbie Hoffman** was found dead on April 12, 1989. Hoffman suffered from bipolar illness, and in his depression he took a lethal dose of 150 phenobarbitals.

2. Harrisburg. Somewhere along the road west of Harrisburg, **Jack Kerouac** met an old withered man he came to call "The Ghost of the Susquehanna." Jack had been hitchhiking from Pittsburgh, probably traveling along **Route 22**, when he was let out on the side of the road. There he met the ghost, who told him to walk with him toward Harrisburg. However, Jack said that the man insisted on walking the wrong way, and Kerouac would have wound up back in Pittsburgh if he had kept at it. "We walked seven miles along the mournful Susquehanna. It is a terrifying river. It has busy cliffs on both sides that lean like hairy ghosts over the unknown waters," he wrote in *On the Road*. Someone finally stopped to give them a lift and the driver tried to tell the ghost that he was still going the wrong direction, but he wouldn't listen. The Ghost of the Susquehanna also figures in Kerouac's posthumously published book *Pic*. The main characters in that book meet up with the ghost under nearly the same circumstances.

3. Muhlenberg. A boyfriend of one of **Allen Ginsberg**'s cousins was a teacher at **Muhlenberg College**, and in 1958 he asked Ginsberg to give a reading there. Allen had made a vow not to accept money for reading poetry, so in lieu of a fee he asked that the college buy poetry books for the school library. The reading was a great success, but the professor was chastised for hosting a "Beatnik."

The following year Gregory Corso, LeRoi Jones, Philip Whalen, and Ray Bremser read at the college, but did not turn down their stipends.

4. Philadelphia.

a. **David Amram** was born in Philadelphia on November 17, 1930, the son of Philip Werner and Emilie Weyl Amram. His father was a lawyer and writer, but when he grew tired of city life he moved his family to a farm in nearby Feasterville.

b. **Sheri Martinelli** was born Shirley Burns Brennan in Philadelphia on January 17, 1918. Her parents, Alphonse and Mae Trindell Brennan, separated while she was still young, and at the beginning of World War II she married Ezio Martinelli, a painter and sculptor. Sheri became a particular favorite and muse of Ezra Pound while he was incarcerated at St. Elizabeth's Hospital in Washington. She was a painter of extremely delicate portraits that appealed to Pound. Her circle of friends included William Gaddis, Allen Ginsberg, Philip Lamantia, and other Beat writers. Pound himself had earned his master's degree in Philadelphia at the **University of Pennsylvania**.

6. Swarthmore.

From 1951 to 1953, **Diane Di Prima** attended **Swarthmore College**, a Quaker school and one of the nation's first coeducational colleges. Di Prima found it too conservative for her tastes and left before graduating. In the 1940s, **Selden Kirby-Smith** (later **Ferlinghetti**), received her B.A. in literature from Swarthmore. She went on to Columbia and wrote her master's thesis on D.H. Lawrence, all before meeting Lawrence Ferlinghetti. **Barney Rosset**, who became the publisher of Grove Press, also went to Swarthmore before World War II. He enrolled there in pursuit of his high school sweetheart, but he left after taking only a few courses. While Rosset was a Swarthmore student, he happened to pick up a copy of Henry Miller's banned book *Tropic of Cancer,* and that changed the course of his life. Years later he was to make a historic and successful defense of its publication in the U.S., overturning old censorship laws.

MIDWEST
REGION

Gregory Corso

III. East North Central States

OHIO

1. Shaker Heights. On May 7, 1963, **Gregory Corso** married a woman from Shaker Heights with the poetic name of **Sally November**. After the birth of their daughter, Miranda, the following year, Sally moved back to a house at **3394 Sutton Road** and landed a teaching job. Corso followed, moving in with his wife and baby. He briefly considered working for Sally's father, who ran a flower shop, and at one point even went to a job interview at a major advertising firm in downtown Cleveland. Alone in the house for most of the day, he suffered a terrible withdrawal from drugs. That same year he was invited to teach at the University of Buffalo. Gregory wrote to his publisher James Laughlin, "G.C. is 34, is wedded, and has baby girl, and must now support souls other than the muse. It should be fun or hell—all the muse needed was a poem—but a wife and daughter, a million dollars." Within a few months, Corso realized that for him, it was hell. Shuttling back and forth to Buffalo killed their relationship, and Corso moved on.

3394 Sutton Road

Photograph by Bill Morgan

2. Cincinnati.

a. **Kenneth Koch** was born in Cincinnati on February 27, 1925. Along with fellow poets John Ashbery and Frank O'Hara, Koch became a prominent member of the New York School. He began writing poems as a young boy when he fell in love with the poetry of Shelley and Keats. Some of his poems make reference to the Ohio River, which he saw as a dividing line between the normal life of Ohio and the wild, uninhibited life of Kentucky. He associated Kentucky with the gambling bars, strip clubs, and brothels that once could be found there. Koch and Allen Ginsberg were friends and often appeared at readings together. They liked to trade poetic lines back and forth and even published a book of their best collaborations, *Making It Up*. Kenneth died on July 6, 2002.

b. Surrealist poet **Howard Hart** was born in Cincinnati on January 23, 1927. At the time the family lived in a large house at **1050 East Rookwood Drive**. Although born in Ohio, Hart lived much of his adult life in New York and San Francisco. He might be best remembered to fans of the Beat Generation for initiating a series of jazz and poetry nights with Jack Kerouac, Philip Lamantia, and David Amram during the late 1950s. Hart passed away in San Francisco on August 10, 2002.

3. Cleveland. When it came time for the **Rock 'n' Roll Hall of Fame** to open its 1997 exhibit, "Let Me Take You Higher: The Psychedelic Era, 1965–1969," the museum asked **Ken Kesey** to round up the **Merry Pranksters** and drive his bus "Further" to the museum. Kesey asked Neal Cassady's son, **John Allen Cassady**, to drive, in commemoration of his father's earlier role as driver. The bus arrived on May 10, just in time for the museum's kick-off party, which featured musical entertainment by the Grateful Dead, The Charlatans, and Big Brother.

4. Columbus. The Rare Books and Manuscripts Library at **Ohio State University** maintains a large part of William S. Burroughs's archive, which is open to scholars. Burroughs began to donate materials to Ohio State before he died in 1997, and his estate has continued that practice.

5. Niles. Kenneth Patchen was born in Niles on December 13, 1911, while the family was living on **Pleasant Street**. His father, Wayne Patchen, worked nearby in the **Youngstown Sheet and Tube** mills, which would later find their way into his poetry. When he was four, his family moved to Warren, Ohio, and Kenneth graduated from the **Warren G. Harding High School at 860 Elm Road N.E.** in 1929. He was admired by many in the Beat Generation not only for his poetry, but also for his political and pacifist views during the 1930s and 1940s. In 1956 Lawrence Ferlinghetti

published Patchen's book *Poems of Humor and Protest*, the third in the City Lights Pocket Poets Series. Ginsberg's *Howl and Other Poems* was the fourth.

6. Oberlin. David Amram attended **Oberlin College** where he studied music under Martin Morris, a member of the Cleveland Symphony Orchestra for one year in 1948–49. Morris tutored Amram in an old-style, scientific German manner, not exactly what the more spontaneous, jazz-loving Amram was hoping for. When David nearly flunked out of school for failing to identify "Calcareous Tufa" on a geology exam, he knew he would not return for a second year.

Shaker Heights (see Ohio location 1).

MICHIGAN

1. Ann Arbor.

a. The **University of Michigan** is a city in itself. Their library boasts one of the country's best special collections departments and houses the papers of many poets including Anne Waldman's archive. Cid Corman was a undergraduate student at Michigan and Frank O'Hara earned his Master's degree here in 1951. Many writers from W.H. Auden to Arthur Miller have been associated with the school and Ted Berrigan taught at the university briefly.

b. The **Jewel Heart Buddhist Center**, at **1129 Oak Valley Drive** is a meditation center founded in 1989 by **Gehlek Rinpoche**. After the 1987 death of his first Buddhist teacher, Chögyam Trungpa Rinpoche, Jewel Heart became an important place of retreat for **Allen Ginsberg**. During the 1990s Ginsberg visited Ann Arbor every year to continue his Tibetan Buddhist training. He often gave benefit readings and performances for Gehlek's group. He was joined by Patti Smith and Philip Glass on several occasions to raise money for Jewel Heart. While on retreat Ginsberg frequently roomed with fellow Buddhist Glass, and together they collaborated on orchestral pieces like *Hydrogen Jukebox* and *Cosmopolitan Greetings*.

2. Detroit.

a. **Jack Kerouac** passed through Detroit many times on his cross-country trips. In 1944, immediately after Jack married **Edie Parker**, he moved to her family's home in Grosse Pointe (see that section), where her father found him a job as a night watchman at the **Fruehauf Trailer Company** in Detroit. Within a month Jack had given up on married life and returned to New York City alone. In the early years he stayed in touch with Edie and often stopped to see her. On one visit he stayed at the **Savarine Hotel**, then at **13115 Jefferson**, where he met several members of the Detroit Tigers baseball team. His Detroit adventures are recorded in Edie's memoir, *You'll Be Okay*, which was published posthumously. The

Edie Kerouac-Parker at home in Detroit

Savarine, no longer a hotel, was renamed the Winston Place Apartments.

In *On the Road* Kerouac mentioned that on one visit to see his ex-wife, Edie's mother wouldn't let him into her house, so he "sat fuming with rage on the floor of the Detroit Greyhound bus station men's room." On that trip Jack had to spend his last few coins on a skid row meal before getting back on the bus. On his next trip to Detroit he and Neal Cassady arrived together by bus and walked five miles up **Mack Avenue** in order to see Edie. When Edie told Jack that if they remarried she'd expect to have a maid, Jack relinquished all thoughts of a reunion with her. Kerouac wasn't pleased with the town after those visits and bitterly wrote, "Detroit is actually one of the worst towns possible in America." In later years, Edie Kerouac-Parker moved to **3549 Bluehill** in Detroit, where she began to work on her memoir.

b. Detroit was the birthplace of jazzman **Slim Gaillard.** Born in 1916 as Bulee Gaillard, he grew up to become a musician admired by both Jack Kerouac and Neal Cassady. Kerouac mentioned him several times in his books, and Slim's scat singing influenced Jack's writing style.

c. Not many Beat memories connected with Detroit were pleasant. **Herbert Huncke** lived in the city for an unhappy period between 1919 and 1921 when he was a small boy. His younger brother, Robert, was born in Detroit just before the family moved to Chicago. As a teenager, Herbert couldn't wait to be free of his family and ran away from home countless times.

d. In 1943, when the poet **Ted Joans** was fifteen years old, his father was killed in a Detroit fight.

3. East Lansing. Carolyn Elizabeth Robinson (later Neal Cassady's second wife) was born in East Lansing on April 28, 1923. She was the youngest of five children born to Dr. Charles S. and Florence Elizabeth Sherwood Robinson, who lived at **272 Bogue Street**, and later at **207 Bogue**. Her father was a member of the chemistry faculty at **Michigan Agricultural College** (now **Michigan State University**), while her mother, a former English teacher, raised the children.

4. Grosse Pointe. Frankie Edith Parker, the first Mrs. Jack Kerouac, was born in Grosse Pointe on September 20, 1922. Baby Edie was delivered at home by her grandfather, Lewis Maire, who was a medical doctor. A local grade school in Grosse Pointe, the **Lewis E. Maire Elementary School** at **740 Cadieux Road**, is named for him. As a teenager Edie attended **Grosse Pointe South High School** at **11 Grosse Pointe Boulevard** in Grosse Pointe Farms. Then, following high school, she moved to her grandmother's apartment in New York City, where she lived while taking

Rustic Cabin Bar

art classes. There she met and married Jack Kerouac. In the late summer of 1944 she and Jack came back to live with her mother and sister at **1407 Somerset Avenue**, also in Grosse Pointe Park. A few blocks from their house is the **Rustic Cabin Bar**, at **15209 Kercheval Street**, where she and Kerouac spent a good deal of their free time. After just a month or so in Grosse Pointe, Jack returned to New York and for all practical purposes their marriage was over. When Kerouac and

1407 Somerset Avenue

Cassady came back to visit Edie in the late 1940s on one of their *On the Road* trips, she was living on the estate of her stepfather, Joseph Berry Sherrard, at **59 Lakeshore Drive**. On that trip the trio hung out at **Pinky's Bar**, which was once on **Jefferson Avenue** across from the Belle Isle Bridge. It was an old-fashioned piano bar that Neal and Jack especially liked. Pinky's is no longer in business, but it is fondly remembered by its clientele. In the years that followed, Edie remarried twice and remained in the Grosse Pointe area for the rest of her life. On October 29, 1993, she died of congestive heart failure at **Bon Secours Hospital**, **468 Cadieux Road**, with her friend and the editor of her memoir, Timothy Moran, at her side.

INDIANA

1. Bloomington.

a. In 1952, after **Gary Snyder**'s graduation from Reed College, he enrolled in graduate school at **Indiana University** at **107 S. Indiana Avenue**. Snyder's classmate from Reed, Dell Hymes, had come to Indiana in 1950 and recommended the school highly. Snyder spent part of a year studying linguistics and anthropology here, but dropped out before earning his graduate degree.

b. **Ted Joans** was a student at **Indiana University** for a brief period in the late 1940s. Ted studied painting, but he did not graduate either.

c. **Alfred Kinsey** was a longtime member of the faculty at the university. In order to gather material for his controversial study of human sexuality in males he visited New York City and met Herbert Huncke on Times Square. That led to interviews with Allen Ginsberg, Jack Kerouac, and William S. Burroughs, and they all became part of the statistics for his 1948 groundbreaking report, *Sexual Behavior in the Human Male*.

d. The university's **Lilly Library** houses one of the nation's great collections of poetry, including rare material by many Beat writers. Researchers at the library can delve into LeRoi Jones's papers for *Yugen* and *The Floating Bear* magazines and pore over the manuscripts of William Carlos Williams.

2. Indianapolis. Jack Kerouac passed through Indianapolis on several of his road trips. In *On the Road* he wrote about a girl he met on a cross-country bus—they "necked all the way to Indianapolis." When they got off the bus, she bought him a meal at a lunch counter because he was penniless, as usual. At that time, the poverty-stricken author could never have imagined that in 2004 the owner of the Indianapolis Colts football team, James Irsay, would purchase the manuscript scroll of *On The Road* for more than $2 million. Since then Irsay has generously lent the scroll to libraries around the world to display.

3. South Bend. Kenneth Rexroth was born in South Bend on December 22, 1905. His parents, Charles and Delia Reed Rexroth, were en route to Chicago at the time. Fifty years later, Rexroth, a father figure and elder statesman to the Beats, was master of ceremonies at the famous Six Gallery reading in San Francisco where Ginsberg, McClure, Snyder, Lamantia, and Whalen read their poetry for the first time.

ILLINOIS

1. Cairo. Ted Joans was born here on July 4, 1928, under the more common spelling of his last name, Theodore Jones. Although he often liked to romanticize his origins and said that his father was a riverboat entertainer and the family lived on board the boat, Ted was actually born

Courtesy of the City Lights Archive

Ted Joans and Alan Ansen

on solid ground. When he grew up Jones changed his surname to Joans in order to set himself apart. It was a romantic start to his life as a poet, musician, and painter. During his seventy-eight years he managed to blend his interests in jazz, poetry, and art into a unique bohemian style all his own. He is best remembered for his slogan "Bird Lives," which he emblazoned on the sidewalks and walls of New York City following Charlie Parker's death in 1955.

2. Charleston. Charleston is the home of **Eastern Illinois University**, one of the many schools where **Ed Dorn** studied briefly. His professor here, Ray Obermayr, was the first to tell Dorn about Black Mountain College, where Ed transferred in 1951 to pursue an interest in painting.

3. Chicago.

a. **Barney Rosset**, the owner of Grove Press and founder of the *Evergreen Review*, was born in Chicago's **Michael Reese Hospital** on May 28, 1922. He lived in eight different places as a boy, among them **2920 Commonwealth Avenue** and **1540 Lake Shore Drive**. His father, the banker Barnet L. Rosset, and his wife Mary sent Barney Jr. to the progressive **Francis W. Parker School** at **330 West Webster Avenue**. After the war Rosset took over tiny Grove Press, which had issued only three books at that time. Rosset made Grove into an influential publishing house and published books by Kerouac, Burroughs, Rechy, and Selby, as well as other groundbreaking authors like Samuel Beckett and Henry Miller. Through Rosset's efforts, Grove Press was successful in challenging America's old censorship laws. It was Rosset who bought the American rights to William Burroughs's *Naked Lunch* and successfully defended it in court against charges of obscenity.

b. **Jackson MacLow** was born in Chicago on September 12, 1922. As a young boy MacLow studied music, and by the age of 15 he was writing poetry. He attended the **University of Chicago** and received an associate's degree in 1941 before moving to New York in 1943. Although not Beat he associated with many of those who were.

c. **James Schuyler,** a Pulitzer Prize–winning poet and a connecting link between the New York School poets and the Beats, was born in Chicago on November 9, 1923, the son of a reporter. His parents, Marcus and Margaret Daisy Connor Schuyler, moved frequently while he was a small boy and divorced when he was still quite young. When James was twelve, he and his mother moved permanently to Buffalo.

d. **Paul Carroll**, the editor of both the *Chicago Review* and *Big Table,* was born in Chicago in 1927. He graduated from the **University of Chicago** with a master's degree in 1952 and became a full professor there, living for a while at **450 West Surf Street**. As one of the editors of the *Chicago Review*, he was an early champion of the Beat writers. When the university moved to suppress an issue of the *Review* that featured the work of William S. Burroughs, Carroll and

Clockwise from top to left: Gregory Corso, Allen Ginsberg, Peter Orlovsky, Paul Carroll in Chicago

95

co-editor Irving Rosenthal founded a new magazine, which they called *Big Table* at Jack Kerouac's suggestion. Carroll founded the Poetry Center of Chicago and went on to edit several influential anthologies and collections of criticism before his death in 1996.

e. Tom Clark was born on the Near West Side of Chicago on March 1, 1941. Clark was raised in Chicago before going to college at the University of Michigan in Ann Arbor. He is the author of a very good biography of Jack Kerouac and played a leading role in the Naropa Poetry Wars waged during the 1980s.

f. The oldest of four children, **Patti Smith** was born in Chicago on December 30, 1946, but spent most of her childhood in Woodbury, New Jersey. Smith became a poet and musician and was a friend of Burroughs, Corso, and Ginsberg. For a while she lived at the Chelsea Hotel in New York City with photographer Robert Mapplethorpe.

Robert Mapplethorpe and Patti Smith

Courtesy of the Allen Ginsberg Trust

g. On **Jack Kerouac**'s first trip across the country in 1947, which he described in *On the Road*, he passed through Chicago. There he found a cheap room at the **YMCA**, and after a good night's sleep, he went out to explore the city: "the wind from Lake Michigan, the beans, bop at the Loop, long walks around So. Halsted and No. Clark." On that visit he was disappointed by the music he heard and said that Chicago jazz sounded worn out. A few years later he returned with Neal Cassady and they caroused through town, visiting the "hootchikootchy joints" on **North Clark Street**. On his second visit Kerouac found the jazz much better. In fact, on that trip Jack and Neal had a chance to hear George Shearing play in person; Shearing was the man Neal referred to famously as "God."

h. **William S. Burroughs** moved to Chicago in the late summer of 1939. He arrived specifically to hear Alfred Korzybski deliver a series of five lectures on his theory of general semantics at the recently founded **Institute of General Semantics**. Korzybski's ideas were a major, if not *the* major, philosophical influence on Burroughs's development. In 1942 William returned to Chicago, lived alone on the North Side, and worked as an exterminator for **A.J. Cohen Exterminators**. He noted that they had a ground-floor office on a dead-end street by the river. Burroughs also worked for **Merritt Inc.**, a detective agency in the city. Both jobs afforded him experiences that would figure prominently in his future writings.

i. In 1920, when he was still a youngster, **Herbert Huncke** moved to **1322 W. Sherwin Avenue**. In Chicago, Herbert's father, Herbert Spencer Huncke, founded H. S. Huncke and Company, a firm distributing machine parts. Before long Herbert's parents separated, and by the time he was fourteen he was living with his mother in an apartment in a wood-frame house on **Superior Street** just east of North State Street. Unhappy at home, he loved to hang out in bohemian neighborhoods like Towertown, the area around the Water Tower on the Near North Side, and there he discovered sex and drugs. He was a troubled teenager and ran away from home several times, never finishing his formal schooling.

j. In 1976, **Philip Lamantia** spent time in Chicago as a participant in the World Surrealist Exhibition, which was organized by Franklin and Penelope Rosemont and held at the **Gallery Black Swan** at **500 North LaSalle Street**. The show included artworks, dance and theater performances, and poetry readings by surrealists from thirty-one countries. **Ted Joans**, another "Beat surrealist," also participated.

k. The **University of Chicago** also figures in the history of the Beat Generation. **Lucien Carr** attended classes here in 1942–43 before he went on to Columbia. In the spring of 1943 Carr tried to commit suicide by putting his head in a gas oven. That landed him in the **Cook County Hospital** for psychological treatment.

In 1958, after the university suppressed the publication of the *Chicago Review*, the editors, **Irving Rosenthal** and **Paul Carroll**, pleaded with Ferlinghetti, Ginsberg, Corso, and Orlovsky to come read at a benefit for their new magazine, *Big Table*. On January 29, 1959, Corso, Ginsberg, and Orlovsky gave a reading under the auspices of the George Bernard Shaw Society at the **Sherman Hotel**, which once stood on the northwest corner of **Randolph and Clark Streets**. Ferlinghetti came too, and read at the **Oriental Theater** at **24 West Randolph Street** later in the year. For Ferlinghetti it was a return to the town where he had gone through naval training. On September 16, 1941, he had been sworn in for midshipmen's school at the **Great Lakes Naval Base** just north of town after enlisting at the Navy's recruiting office at **111 East Pearson Street**.

Lew Welch went to graduate school at the **University of Chicago** in the early 1950s. To support himself he took various jobs, at first working for the post office. From time to time his old Reed classmate Gary Snyder visited him from Bloomington, where Gary was studying anthropology in graduate school from 1952 to 1953. During his Chicago years, Welch suffered a nervous breakdown, which interrupted his studies. Lew stayed in Chicago for several years, employed in marketing and finally as an ad copywriter for **Montgomery Ward and Co.** until he left for California in 1957. Welch wrote a poem titled "Chicago Poem" that begins: "I lived here nearly 5 years before I could / meet the middle western day with anything approaching / Dignity. It's a place that lets you / understand why the Bible is the way it is: / Proud people cannot live here. . . ."

l. In 1968, Chicago became the focus of national attention when the Democrats held their presidential convention in the city. *Esquire* magazine hired Allen Ginsberg, William S. Burroughs, Jean Genet, and Terry Southern to cover the event. Ginsberg stayed at the **Sheraton Hotel, 301 East North Water Street**, at the magazine's expense, but he became part of the story when he joined the antiwar demonstrators in what he hoped would be peaceful rallies. After a week of civil disobedience and police violence, the organizers, collectively known as the Chicago Eight, were charged with inciting a riot. Ginsberg returned to Chicago the following year to testify at the trial of Rennie Davis, David Dellinger, John Froines, Tom Hayden, Abbie Hoffman, Jerry Rubin, and Lee Weiner. One defendant, Bobby Seale, was tried separately. Ginsberg shocked the judge by chanting the mantra "Om" in an attempt to foster a meditative atmosphere in the courtroom, just as he had during the Grant Park demonstrations.

Courtesy of the Allen Ginsberg Trust

Clockwise from top left: Jean Genet, Allen Ginsberg, and Terry Southern viewing the Democratic National Convention from the balcony

4. Joliet. When **Jack Kerouac** left Chicago on his 1947 trip to Denver, he took a bus as far as Joliet, just past the prison. Then he walked through Joliet's "leafy rickety streets" and when he reached the outskirts of town, he stuck out his thumb and began to hitchhike west. His first ride was on a dynamite truck.

5. Lockport. In 1940 while living in Chicago, **William S. Burroughs** enrolled in the **Lewis School of Aviation (now Lewis University)** on **Airport Road** in nearby Lockport. If he earned his pilot's license, Burroughs hoped it would help him when he applied for various officer's training programs. Although he passed flight school and received his license, he never became an officer in the military.

6. Rock Island. Hitching rides to Denver in 1947, **Jack Kerouac** passed through Rock Island and it was here that he saw the Mississippi River for the first time. "Dry in the summer haze, low-water, with its big rank smell that smells like the raw body of America itself," he wrote in *On the Road.*

7. Villa Grove. Edward Dorn was born in Villa Grove on April 2, 1929. There he received his earliest education in a one-room schoolhouse. Following high school Dorn went to the University of Illinois in Urbana and several other colleges before finally joining Robert Creeley and Charles Olson as one of the Black Mountain College poets. Dorn's first book, *The Newly Fallen,* was published in 1961 by LeRoi Jones's Totem Press.

WISCONSIN

1. Appleton. In February 1968 **Allen Ginsberg** gave a reading in Appleton with **The Fugs**, the outrageous rock group formed by poets Tuli Kupferberg, Ed Sanders, and Ken Weaver. The following day they led about seventy-five people to **St. Mary's Cemetery** at **1200 Racine Road**

in Menasha. There they performed an exorcism at the grave of Senator Joseph McCarthy, the politician who had conducted a Communist witch-hunt in the early 1950s as head of the Tydings Committee.

2. Land O' Lakes. In the fall of 1976, **Chögyam Trungpa** organized a three-month Buddhist retreat in Land O' Lakes. About a hundred meditation students, including **Allen Ginsberg** and **Peter Orlovsky**, filled the venerable **Kings Gateway Hotel, 4103 Highway B**, which was otherwise closed for the season. Ginsberg loved both the discipline of sitting meditation and the healthy regimen that Trungpa enforced during his retreats. Even though he was on retreat, Ginsberg managed to write poems like "Land O'Lakes, Wisc." and "Land O'Lakes, Wisconsin: Vajrayana Seminary."

3. Madison.

a. Poet **Paul Blackburn** graduated from the **University of Wisconsin** in Madison in 1949. Following college he returned to New York City where he wrote poetry and organized numerous readings.

b. Antler, a poet and naturalist, attended the **University of Wisconsin** for a while but left before graduation. Allen Ginsberg admired Antler's poetry and helped convince Lawrence Ferlinghetti to publish Antler's *Factory* in the Pocket Poets Series. "*Factory* inspired me to laughter near tears, I think it's the most enlightening and magnanimous American poem I've seen since *Howl* of my own generation," Ginsberg wrote.

Antler

Dave Haselwood, Lee Streiff, and Michael McClure in Wichita

IV. West North Central States

KANSAS

1. Marysville. The prairie states were not only traversed countless times by Neal Cassady and Jack Kerouac during their cross-country jaunts, but were also home to several Beat Generation writers. Poet **Michael McClure** was born in Marysville on October 20, 1932, to Thomas and Marian Dixie Johnston McClure. Michael has vivid memories of the cast-iron lions near the **Koester House** at **10th and Broadway** in Marysville and spent weeks on a nearby farm watching cows being milked by hand.

    Allen Ginsberg mentioned the town in his poem "Wichita Vortex Sutra," and he was thinking about the McClures of Marysville when he wrote about the "grandfathers of Kansas" in "Howl."

2. Dodge City. Dennis Hopper, an actor with ties to the Beat Generation, was born in Dodge City on

May 17, 1936. His parents moved to San Diego when he was a boy and he grew up there. In 1954 he went to Hollywood to become an actor and starred in dozens of movies, including *Rebel Without a Cause* and *Easy Rider,* directing the latter as well. While living in Los Angeles he became associated with a group of artists and writers that included Wallace Berman, David Meltzer, and Michael McClure. In addition to his acting career, Hopper was also a distinguished photographer and had many exhibitions of his work before his death in 2010.

3. Holcomb. On April 26, 1935, writer **Charles Plymell** was born in Holcomb on the Finney County high plains. He was younger than many Beat writers and might best be called a member of the "post-beat" generation. In college Plymell worked for a printer and later used the skills he learned to publish books under the imprint Cherry Valley Editions.

4. Lawrence. In 1981 **William S. Burroughs** moved permanently to the college town of Lawrence. For a year he lived in a small stone house until November 1982 when he moved to **1927 Learnard Street**. Here he lived for the next fifteen years until his death on August 2, 1997, in **Lawrence Memorial Hospital**. During those years his friends often stopped to visit him whenever they were in Kansas. In addition to writing, Burroughs created imaginative artworks, some made by splattering paint onto a canvas with a blast

James Grauerholz and William S. Burroughs

from one of his firearms. Although he had tortured cats when he was younger, Burroughs became a cat lover in later years. Ten of his cats, including Ruski, his favorite, are buried in the backyard "cat cemetery." Ruski became the subject of a small chapbook of the same name that Burroughs published. In 2004 the house was added to the Lawrence Register of Historic Places, and it is hoped that someday it may be open to the public. In honor of the writer's residence, the nearby creek has been renamed Burroughs Creek.

Burroughs moved to Lawrence to be close to his friend **James Grauerholz**. Born in Coffeyville, Kansas, Grauerholz attended the University of Kansas from 1969 until he dropped out in 1973, the year he went to New York and met Ginsberg and Burroughs. After acting as Burroughs's personal secretary for a decade, Grauerholz decided to return home to Kansas and Burroughs followed.

The **University of Kansas** has always been a magnet for the Beats. Even before Burroughs moved to Lawrence, Allen Ginsberg read at the university, including one tour in 1966 when he was filmed by photographer Robert Frank for Frank's movie *Me and My Brother*.

Bruce Conner and Dennis Hopper

5. McPherson. Artist **Bruce Conner** was born in McPherson on November 18, 1933, and lived there until he was about four years old. Then his family moved to Wichita, where he attended school with Michael McClure and formed a lifelong friendship with the poet.

Marysville (see Kansas location 1).

6. Wichita.

a. Wichita was the most important stop on **Allen Ginsberg**'s February 1966 tour. Here he spent some of his time at the **Magic Theatre/Vortex Art Gallery** at **625 Douglas**, next to the Eaton Hotel at the railroad overpass. The Magic Theatre had formerly been known as Moody Connell's Skidrow Beanery, but Allen co-opted the vortex idea to show that Kansas was geographically and ideologically in the center of the nation. His long poem "Wichita Vortex Sutra" is wonderfully detailed in local specifics. Ginsberg came to Kansas because Charles Plymell, a Kansas native and a friend of Allen's in San Francisco, had arranged for the reading tour.

b. **Michael McClure** moved back to Wichita in 1941 when he was still a young boy. He attended **Robinson Junior High, 328 North Oliver Street** and then **East High School, 2301 East Douglas Avenue**, but he admitted to skipping classes as often as he could. Instead of doing his course work he read a great deal and discovered Emanuel Swedenborg, Jacob Boehme, and modern poetry in the public library. In Wichita McClure made friends with future artists **Dave Haselwood, Bruce Conner,** and **Bob Branaman**. In 1951 Michael began his freshman year at the **University of Wichita** before transferring to Arizona in 1953. Michael's novel *Mad Cub* is based on his early life in Wichita, but he relocated the story in Tulsa. Thanks to Lee Streiff, author of the essay "The Beat Vortex," we know that McClure lived at **612 North Belmont Street** from 1945 to 1949; at **610 South Beverly Drive** from 1949 to 1951; and then at **1723 North Holyoke Street** in 1951–52.

c. Not surprisingly, **Jack Kerouac** passed through Wichita, too, on one of his *On the Road* journeys. During a layover at the bus station Jack went to the bathroom, where he was propositioned by a minister's son wearing a loud herringbone suit. "What a sad Sunday night for the Kansas minister's son; what Wichita doldrums," he lamented.

NEBRASKA

1. Grand Island. In *On the Road*, **Jack Kerouac's** alter ego, Sal Paradise, and Eddie, his hitchhiking partner at the time, helped a cowboy drive

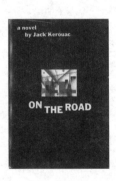

his car to Grand Island. There the man had to turn off and head north toward Montana. Their next ride was a short one with some country boys in a put-together jalopy, and from there they got a ride as far as Preston with a silent old man, driving across the plains in a light drizzle.

2. Lincoln. In 1966, when **Allen Ginsberg** was making his tour of "the vortex," he read in Lincoln before a huge crowd of three thousand fans. The police monitored his performance and prepared to close it down in case he said anything "obscene." Ginsberg's Kansas friend, **Charles Plymell**, had put together a series of half a dozen readings around the area. Ginsberg was at the height of his fame, and *Life* magazine covered the tour in an article they titled

"The Guru Comes to Kansas." Their reporter described Allen as a "wild haired wild man."

3. North Platte. When one of **Jack Kerouac**'s rides left him off in North Platte, he didn't realize that he was about to have the "greatest ride" of his life. A flatbed truck with five boys in the back, driven by two blond farmers from Minnesota, pulled over to pick him up and he climbed aboard. As they rode wildly through the night, Jack took swigs of rotgut that the boys were passing around and hung on to the truck for dear life. All the riders were from different parts of the country—Ohio, Montana, the Dakotas, and Mississippi—an impromptu fraternity of young men on the move.

4. Ogallala. On the tumultuous truck ride from North Platte, the drivers stopped for a few minutes in Ogallala. The two boys from Dakota got off and went to look for harvesting jobs while **Jack Kerouac** went into a lonely soda fountain for cigarettes. Back on the truck it began to get cold, so the remaining riders huddled together under the huge tarpaulin used to cover farm machinery and finished off their bottle of cheap booze.

Jack Kerouac

5. Omaha. On his first trip to Denver to see Neal Cassady, **Jack Kerouac** teamed up with a hitchhiker named Eddie, a partner he described in great detail in *On the Road*. Kerouac liked him, so when they couldn't get a lift, Jack was generous enough to pay for both their bus tickets to Omaha. As they pulled into town, Kerouac was thrilled to see his very first cowboy. He thought he looked as beat as anyone in New York City, except that the cowboy was wearing a ten-gallon hat and Texas boots. After Jack and Eddie got off the bus at the depot, they walked up a hill and out of town to begin thumbing again. That's when a cowboy asked them to drive his car to Grand Island. For the next hundred miles they followed the Platte River, which a rancher had once told Jack was as great as the Valley of the Nile. When he saw it for himself he had to agree.

6. Shelton. One of the drivers who gave **Jack Kerouac** and Eddie a ride left them out along the road in Shelton, just across the railroad tracks from the town water tank. Jack reported that the name of the town was written in big letters on the side of the tank. In *On the Road,* Kerouac calls the town Preston, which seems odd, because Preston is actually hundreds of miles away in the southeast corner of the state. Eddie said he had been in Shelton before and didn't like it, and on this trip they became stranded there. As it got damp and cold, Jack gave Eddie his wool plaid shirt to wear and caught a cold himself. He also bought some penny postcards and mailed them from the tiny post office. (A little research reveals that a postcard to his mother was mailed from Shelton, so it does seem unlikely that the scene took place in Preston.) The local sheriff spotted them and offered them work in a little traveling carnival on the edge of town, but, eager to move on, they both declined. Before long a man stopped, but said he had room for only one of them. As a result, Eddie selfishly jumped into the truck, leaving Jack behind. Even worse for Jack was that Eddie forgot to return Jack's warm plaid shirt before disappearing down the highway.

7. Sidney. On August 1, 1946, **Neal Cassady** married **LuAnne Henderson** in Denver. The following month they stayed briefly with her aunt and uncle in Sidney, Nebraska. The newlyweds planned to support themselves by picking potatoes, and Neal also considered washing dishes in a local restaurant. When those ideas fell through, LuAnne took a job as a housemaid for a wealthy lawyer, **Radcliffe Moore**, who lived on **Linden Street** in Sidney. The Moores allowed LuAnne and Neal to live in the tiny maid's room of the house, but the work was difficult and LuAnne resented being treated like a servant. That October, she took $300 from the lawyer's desk and some books from his study and escaped to North Platte in her uncle's car, which Neal had just stolen. There they ditched the car and hopped on a bus, using the lawyer's money to pay for their first trip to New York City, the trip on which they were to meet Kerouac, Ginsberg, and the rest.

MINNESOTA

1. Duluth. Many people know that the most famous native son of Duluth is **Robert Allen Zimmerman**, better known as **Bob Dylan**. He was born on May 24, 1941, and lived in Duluth at **519 North Third Avenue East** until he was nearly seven. Later he adopted the name Dylan in honor of Dylan Thomas. He was attracted to poetry in general and the Beats in particular. When he moved to New York in early 1961, he met Allen Ginsberg, Gregory Corso, and Ray Bremser and became friendly with them and other poets around Greenwich Village.

Bob Dylan and Allen Ginsberg

2. Hibbing. After they left Duluth, Hibbing became the new home for **Bob Dylan** and his family. In 1947, when Bob was seven, the Zimmermans moved to Hibbing to be closer to his mother's family. His father, Abe Zimmerman, had been stricken with polio and was able to work in her family's appliance store on Fifth Avenue. Bob grew up in an old gray house at **2425 Seventh Avenue East**. He attended the beautiful "Castle in the Woods," as **Hibbing High School** at **801 East 21st Street** was called, and graduated in 1959. While in high school Dylan formed several amateur bands, including The Shadow Blasters and The Golden Chords, which performed in the school's talent shows. He also discovered a copy of Kerouac's *Mexico City Blues* and dreamed of escaping from the conformity of the Midwest.

3. Minneapolis.

a. For a little more than a year, from September 1959 until the end of 1960, Bob Zimmerman attended the **University of Minneapolis**, now part of the **University of Minnesota**. It was while he was living in Minneapolis that he adopted his stage name, **Bob Dylan**.

b. Minneapolis's **Hazelden Foundation** was recommended to **Allen Ginsberg** as a good place for his companion **Peter Orlovsky** to undergo alcohol- and substance-abuse rehabilitation. Ginsberg wasn't able to convince Orlovsky to go through detox voluntarily, but Allen and Peter's girlfriend, Beverly Isis, attended the Family Service and Therapy Program at the Hazelden Center in the fall of 1987 to learn more about addiction and codependency. That proved to be of some help to Ginsberg who was always guilty of "enabling."

c. **Gregory Corso** spent the last months of his life in Minnesota with his daughter, **Sheri Baird**. Sheri was the child born to Boni Pedersen after she had a brief romance with Corso in Los Angeles during the early 1950s. Corso didn't even know he had a daughter by Boni until Sheri was able to locate him in 1984. In September 2000, as Gregory entered the final stages of cancer, Sheri invited him to Minnesota to be with her at the end. She was a trained nurse and generously took care of Corso in her home on **Sumter Circle** in Brooklyn Park just outside of Minneapolis. In January Gregory's condition worsened and he was admitted to the hospice unit of the **North Memorial Medical Center, 3300 Oakdale Avenue North** in Robbinsdale, Minnesota, where he died peacefully a few days later on January 17, 2001.

IOWA

1. Adel. Under an elm tree at a gas station in this small town **Jack Kerouac** met a fellow hitchhiker named Eddie who, like Jack, was on his way to Denver. Eddie had nothing with him except a toothbrush and a handkerchief. They struck out together, but Kerouac soon realized that he should have gone on alone and described their awkward trip in *On the Road*.

2. Cherokee. Donald Allen was born in 1912 and grew up in a large Iowa family. His father, Paul Allen, was a medical doctor who lived in a house at **536 Bailey Court**. As an adult Allen became an erudite and astute editor. He put together a groundbreaking anthology of poetry for Grove Press in 1960 *The New American Poetry 1945–1960,* that linked many Beat writers with the Black Mountain

and New York School poets. When Barney Rosset founded the *Evergreen Review* in 1957, Don Allen became its editor, and later went on to publish Snyder, Whalen, Welch, Ginsberg, and Lamantia under his own imprints, Grey Fox Press and Four Seasons Foundation. Allen died in San Francisco on August 29, 2004.

3. Council Bluffs. As a boy, **Jack Kerouac** had heard tales about the great wagon trains that gathered at Council Bluffs to begin their trek across the plains to California. On first seeing the town for himself, he was disappointed. "Of course now it was only cute suburban cottages of one damn dumb kind and another, all laid out in the dismal gray dawn," he wrote in *On the Road*. It wasn't until he crossed the Missouri River into Nebraska that he saw his first cowboy and was cheered up.

4. Davenport. Iowa stood right in the middle of many of the cross-country trips that several Beat writers made from New York to Denver and San Francisco. On his first trip to Denver in 1947, a truck driver that **Jack Kerouac** was riding with pulled his rig over to sleep for a few hours in a small Iowa town. Possibly it was near Grinnell, but in any case it was east of Des Moines. While the trucker slept, Jack walked around the town with "the prairie brooding at the end of each little street and the smell of corn like dew in the night." It was a better experience than the time a few years later when he and **Neal Cassady** were pulled over by the local police in the same area. The patrolman suspected them of driving a stolen Cadillac, but fortunately it was a drive-away car, and the car's owner in Chicago vouched for them via phone.

On that earlier trip to Denver, Kerouac traversed the state on **Route 6**, eating mostly apple pie and ice cream along the way. Coming out of Davenport he caught a short ride and was left off at "a lonely crossroads on the edge of the prairie." It was a beautiful spot, but he couldn't get another ride and was afraid he would be stranded along the road in the middle of night. His luck prevailed and he was offered a ride back into downtown Davenport. From there he caught another ride at a busy truck stop.

5. Des Moines.

a. On one trip through Des Moines, **Jack Kerouac**, looking for a cheap room, found the local **YMCA** filled, so he headed for the rundown district near the railroad tracks. Without much trouble he found a dilapidated old hotel. Jack slept the whole day in the dingy room there, having come halfway across the country without stopping to rest. While in the gloomy hotel room he had one of the strangest moments of his life when he awoke and realized that he didn't know who he was and wondered just what he was doing there. "I wasn't scared," he wrote afterwards, "I was just somebody else, some stranger, and my whole life was a haunted life." After his usual meal of apple pie and ice cream his spirits returned and he began eyeing the beautiful girls who were going home from school. "The prettiest girls in the world live in Des Moines, Iowa," he noted in *On the Road*.

b. Before **Neal Cassady** was born in 1926, his father was a barber in Des Moines. In 1919 Neal Sr. lived at **931 Seventh Street** and in 1921 at **207½ Sixth Avenue**.

6. Iowa City. The **University of Iowa** dominates the town of Iowa City. Iowa native **Donald Allen** received his undergraduate and master's degree in English from Iowa in 1935. His thesis was titled "Expressionism in American Drama." After graduation Allen became a college professor at a Catholic school in Davenport, but left to serve in military intelligence during World War II. Later he would settle in New York, where he became an editor at Grove Press.

7. Stuart. On the first of his many trips to Denver, **Jack Kerouac**, traveling with a fellow hitchhiker named Eddie, was stranded in Stuart, Iowa. They realized that if they had known how to hop a moving freight train they could have made good time across the plains, but instead they had to go by bus as far as Omaha. This is a tale retold in some detail in *On the Road*.

MISSOURI

1. Kansas City.

a. Sitting in a Kansas City bar on **Market Street** in March 1947, **Neal Cassady** wrote what became known as "The Great Sex Letter." Cassady was in town on a bus layover, heading back to Denver. In the letter addressed to Jack Kerouac, Neal told of his seduction of two women during the trip. The free-flowing letter helped convince Kerouac that there was something naturally unrepressed and free about Cassady and his uninhibited attitude. Kerouac was always shy and timid, especially when it came to women, and this letter reinforced the notion that Neal was his polar opposite.

Neal Cassady

b. In 1933, **Stan Brakhage** was born Robert Sanders, to a woman in a home for unwed mothers in Kansas City. When he was three weeks old, he was adopted by Ludwig and Clara Brakhage and given the name James Stanley Brakhage. His adoptive parents were not well matched, and they divorced when he was six. At that time Clara relocated to Denver, and Brakhage grew up there. During the 1960s Stan became well known as one of America's leading avant-garde filmmakers, influenced in part by the literary works of Robert Duncan and Gertrude Stein. During this period he became close to poets Robert Creeley, Allen Ginsberg, Michael McClure, and Charles Olson. His experimental films, like his *Dog Star Man* cycle, drew the ire of censors, due in large part to some nude footage. In response, Allen Ginsberg helped form a committee of writers to champion First Amendment rights and put a stop to the harassment of underground films.

c. **Edward Sanders** was born on August 17, 1939, in Kansas City. His parents were Lyle and Mollie Cravens Sanders. As a boy Ed was raised in **Blue Springs**, just east of Kansas City, where he took piano lessons, studied drums with the percussionist from the Kansas City Philharmonic, and sang in school productions. The Sanders's home was a red brick house designed by his mother near the bottom of Cemetery Hill, the inspiration for an early poem of his called "Cemetery Hill." While living in Blue Springs, Ed's mother instilled in him a love for literature, especially the Greek and Latin classics. As a sixteen-year-old, Sanders often drove into Kansas City to hear jazz at a place called **Jazznocracy** and to dance away the nights. In the autumn of 1957, just after the death of his mother, Sanders enrolled in the **University of Missouri** in Columbia but dropped out in 1958 to head for New York City. While at college in Missouri, Sanders first read Ginsberg's "Howl," which he credits with changing his life. "An epochal event," he later recalled.

2. St. Louis.

a. The city of St. Louis was the birthplace of several remarkable members of the Beat Generation. On February 5, 1914, **William S. Burroughs** was born in his parent's three-story brick house at **4664 Pershing Avenue** in the city's West End neighborhood. Burroughs's mother, Laura Lee, was the author of several books on flower arranging, and his father, Mortimer (Mote), ran his own business. They were well-off financially, but Burroughs was always quick to point out that his family was not as wealthy as people assumed, even though he was the grandson of the man who had invented the adding machine. Still, the Burroughs family was solidly middle class, and their house was a handsome one with fancy wrought-iron gates on a tree-lined block. Today this gated community is what the locals call a "private place," meaning that only residents have a key to enter the street.

In 1926 Burroughs's parents sold their Pershing Avenue home and built a new white frame house on five acres of land at **700 South Price Road** in suburban Ladue. William was twelve when they moved in, and it was in the new house that he had many memorable boyhood adventures. In 1929 he suffered severe burns to his hand when his chemistry set exploded, and he remembered being thankful for the large dose of morphine the doctor administered. While living in Ladue, Laura and Mote opened **Cobblestone Gardens**, a gift and antique shop then at **10036 Conway Road**. Much later, in 1976, Burroughs used that name as the title for one of his short books, *Cobble Stone Gardens*.

William S. Burroughs' birthplace, 4664 Pershing Avenue

As a teenager William Burroughs went to the **John Burroughs School**, still located just across the street from his home. (See the Burroughs School entry below.) In 1929 he was sent away to a boarding school in New Mexico for a few years, but returned to St. Louis before graduating. In order to receive his high school diploma, Burroughs had to enroll in the **Taylor School** at **222 North Central Avenue**, from which he graduated in

1932. He was always an excellent student and had no trouble getting in to Harvard. Years later Burroughs enlisted in the U.S. Army (although he later claimed that he was drafted). In the spring of 1942 he reported to the **Jefferson Barracks** just outside St. Louis for basic training. Army life didn't suit him, so his mother sent him to see Dr. David Rioch, a psychiatrist, who helped him secure a discharge from the military after Burroughs had served for four or five months.

When Burroughs's only brother, **Mortimer Burroughs Jr.**, married, he and his wife **Miggy** bought a house at **6617 Pershing Avenue** near his parents' old house in the West End. In 1951, shortly after William Burroughs accidentally shot and killed his wife, Joan Vollmer Adams, their four-year-old son, **Billy Jr.**, was dropped off here by Joan's parents to live with Mort and Miggy. Before long the couple realized they couldn't cope with the troubled boy, so Billy was put in the custody of his grandparents, growing up first at the South Price Road house and later in Florida.

Like Hollywood, St. Louis has a Walk of Fame with brass stars and plaques devoted to notable residents. During Burroughs's lifetime, his star was placed on the sidewalk in front of **6362 Delmar Boulevard**.

On August 2, 1997, William Burroughs died in Kansas and his body was brought to the family plot in St. Louis's **Bellefontaine Cemetery, 4947 W. Florissant Avenue**, in keeping with his wishes. He was laid to rest alongside his famous grandfather, the inventor; his uncle Horace, the drug addict; and his parents. His son Billy's name

Burroughs family marker

Photograph by Bill Morgan

is also inscribed on the family marker, but his remains are not here. William's marker is a modest headstone next to the large obelisk erected for his grandfather by the Burroughs Adding Machine Company. Fellow St. Louis native and friend **David Kammerer** was buried in the same cemetery following his 1944 murder.

b. **Lucien Carr** was born in New York on March 1, 1925, but raised in St. Louis. He is not as well known as Burroughs, but his influence on the early Beat group was nearly as great. Carr was an outgoing student at Columbia, and it was through Lucien that Jack Kerouac met Allen Ginsberg and William Burroughs. While living in St. Louis with his mother, Marion Gratz, Carr joined a Boy Scout troop whose scoutmaster was David Kammerer, described below.

c. **David Kammerer** was born in 1911 and grew up at **738 Central Avenue** in Clayton, a wealthy suburb of St. Louis, with his parents Alfred and Laura Kammerer and brother Richard. David's father was an engineer who had moved from **3406 Lindell Boulevard** in St. Louis shortly after his son's birth. Kammerer was also sent to the **John Burroughs School**, where he was a classmate of Burroughs's older brother Mort. It was through Mort that David met William. After high school Kammerer attended **Washington University** from 1930 to 1934 and went on to teach classes there. Obsessed with Lucien Carr, who was fourteen years

David Kammerer, high school yearbook

his junior, Kammerer left his position at the college and followed the boy around the country, eventually winding up in New York City. His homosexual fixation led ultimately to David's death when Lucien murdered him in the summer of 1944, the result of his aggressive sexual advances.

d. **Kells Elvins** was William Burroughs's oldest and closest friend. He was the same age as William and as a baby lived with his father, an attorney named Politte Elvins, and mother at **220 Church Street** in St. Francois, Perry, Missouri. His family also moved to Price Road in the St. Louis suburbs, where he and Burroughs became classmates at the John Burroughs School. After high school they both attended Harvard, and they later bought farmland together in south Texas.

e. The **John Burroughs School** at **755 South Price Road** was named after John Burroughs the naturalist, no relation to **William S. Burroughs**. It catered to students from the upper-middle-class suburbs around Ladue/Clayton. William went there from 1925 until 1929, as did **David Kammerer**, who graduated in 1929. Burroughs's first published work, an essay titled "Personal Magnetism," appeared in the February 1929 issue of the school magazine, the *John Burroughs Review*. More than a decade later **Lucien Carr** was to graduate from the same school.

f. Later, in the 1940s, **Jack Kerouac** laid over in St. Louis for a few hours on one of his many bus trips across the country. On that occasion he wrote about walking down to the **Mississippi River** at noon to see the old steamboats moored at the docks. There he watched logs from the great northern forests floating past on their way down the river and dreamed of taking a Huck Finn–style raft trip himself.

g. **Jay Landesman**, the founder and editor of *Neurotica* magazine, was born in St. Louis in 1919. *Neurotica*'s contributors included Carl Solomon, Allen Ginsberg, and John Clellon Holmes. Jay and his wife, Fran, also owned the hippest nightclub in town, the **Crystal Palace**, once at **4240 Oliver Street**. Landesman's life among the bohemians inspired a Broadway play called *The Nervous Set* and is documented in his own tell-all memoir, *Rebel Without Applause.*

h. **Stuart Z. Perkoff** was born in St. Louis on July 29, 1930. He was one of three sons of Nat and Ann Perkoff. His father was a telegraph operator, and the family lived at **5917 Theodosis Avenue**. Stuart is most often associated with the Beat group living in the Venice Beach neighborhood of Los Angeles made famous in Lawrence Lipton's book *The Holy Barbarians.* Perkoff is often thought of as the quintessential Beatnik. His poems, written on the walls of the Venice West Coffeehouse, which he founded, inspired many wanna-be poets. At the time of his death on June 24, 1974, he was only 43.

3. Unionville. Neal Marshall Cassady, Neal's father, was born in Unionville on September 7, 1893. In June 1932, six-year-old Neal and his father spent a few months in town visiting Eva Jones, Neal Sr.'s sister.

SOUTH DAKOTA

1. Mt. Rushmore. In the summer of 1959 **Allen Ginsberg** and **Peter Orlovsky** went to a car agency in New Mexico, where they had gone to visit Robert Creeley. They were hired to drive a car back to New York and took advantage of the opportunity to spend some time leisurely driving along Route 85, touring the foothills of the Rockies and stopping at some of the places they had always wanted to see. One of these spots was Mt. Rushmore, whose massive stone portraits impressed them, and they drove through the Black Hills and Badlands enjoying the countryside like so many other tourists before and after them.

2. Sioux Falls. During World War II, **Philip Whalen** was sent to the **Army Air Force Training Command Technical School** in Sioux Falls. He spent about two months on the base learning the fundamentals of Morse Code and radio repair.

NORTH DAKOTA

1. Dickinson. In 1949 as he was on his way back from the West Coast with fifteen baloney sandwiches in his knapsack, **Jack Kerouac**'s bus cut across the northern tier of the country and passed over icy roads through North Dakota snowdrifts. Finally, a mile outside of Dickinson, the snow fell so hard that it made the road impassable and the bus had to stop. Most of the passengers waited in a diner for the snowplows to clear the road, but Jack, who loved cold weather, stretched out in the back of the bus and slept.

2. Fargo.
a. After being pulled out of another snowdrift, the bus **Jack Kerouac** was riding from San Francisco to New York had to stop for repairs. They pulled into a Fargo garage where the mechanics were able to fix the problem quickly.
b. Fargo was the birthplace of poet **Madeline Gleason**. She was born there in 1903, the only child of Irish Catholic parents who sent her to the Catholic school in town. Gleason was an influential literary figure and is remembered as one of the founders of the Poetry Center at San Francisco State University. The Center has supported and documented the city's poetry scene from the San Francisco Renaissance to the present. Gleason passed away in 1979.

City Lights in North Dakota. Left to right, top: Michael McClure, Gregory Corso, Miriam Patchen, Kenneth Rexroth, Allen Ginsberg, Lawrence Ferlinghetti. Bottom: unknown, Joanna McClure, unknown, Shig Murao, Jane McClure, Gary Snyder, Peter Orlovsky

3. Grand Forks. One of the first academic conferences to treat the Beat Generation seriously was held at the **University of North Dakota** in Grand Forks March 18–22, 1974, under the auspices of the English Department. The conference, called "City Lights in North Dakota," featured panels and discussions with Gregory Corso, Michael McClure, Miriam Patchen, Kenneth Rexroth, Allen Ginsberg, Lawrence Ferlinghetti, Shig Murao, Gary Snyder, and Peter Orlovsky in attendance. It helped promote a scholarly approach to the Beat Generation.

SOUTH
REGION

LeRoi Jones and Allen Ginsberg

V. South Atlantic States

DISTRICT OF COLUMBIA

a. **LeRoi Jones** attended **Howard University, 2400 Sixth Street N.W.**, from 1952 to 1954. There he studied English, philosophy, religion, and German. In February 1959, Jones returned to Washington to give readings at Howard and Geroge Washington universities. He brought some of his new friends with him: Allen Ginsberg, Gregory Corso, and Ray Bremser. It was on that trip that Bremser met and fell in love with his future wife, Bonnie Frazer, at a reading given in the **Odd Fellows Hall**. They were married three weeks later on March 21, 1959.

b. **Brenda "Bonnie" Frazer** was born in suburban Washington, D.C., on July 23, 1939. She was the daughter of a State Department employee and spent her childhood in the capital. After graduating from high school in Washington in 1959 she enrolled at Sweet Briar College, but left to travel with poet Ray Bremser and never returned to school.

c. **St. Elizabeth's Hospital.** From 1946 to 1958, **Ezra Pound** was detained in St. Elizabeth's, a federally run psychiatric hospital, at **2700 Martin Luther King Avenue S.E.** During World War II, Pound had lived in Italy and was outspoken in his support of Mussolini and the Fascists, denouncing the Allies over Italian radio. After the war he was held in this hospital instead of being sent to prison. It was wiser to regard him as a madman rather than a traitor. Pound was allowed to receive visitors, and Diane Di Prima, Sheri Martinelli, Charles Olson, William Carlos Williams, and Louis Zukofsky made trips to see him. When Allen Ginsberg tried to visit in 1953, Ezra refused, telling William Carlos Williams to keep his own crazy friends to himself. St. Elizabeth's, which officially was called the Government Hospital for the Insane, is now the headquarters for the Department of Homeland Security.

Ezra Pound, Allen Ginsberg, and Nanda Pivano in Italy

Photograph by Ettore Sottsass

d. During the sixties the nation's capital was the epicenter for many protests aimed at stopping the Vietnam War. In March 1967, poet **Ed Sanders** led a march on the **Pentagon** with the intention of exorcising the demons at work there. **Abbie Hoffman** came to Washington on his own mission to levitate the Pentagon building itself. In May 1970, **Allen Ginsberg** marched to the **Washington Monument** as part of the Mobilization Against the War, but the war continued in spite of all their efforts.

e. Jack Kerouac passed through the nation's capital many times. One important encounter with Al Hinkle, Neal Cassady, and LuAnne Henderson was described in *On the Road.* The four of them arrived in Washington on Truman's inauguration day, January 20, 1949. Before the parade began, they checked out all the displays of military weaponry that lined **Pennsylvania Avenue**. Later that day, on their way out of town they found themselves lost on a circular roadway which Kerouac swore was designed to have no exit except into a restaurant's parking lot.

f. The Poetry Consultant for the **Library of Congress** from 1956 until 1958 was writer **Randall Jarrell**. Gregory Corso first met Jarrell in San Francisco in 1956, and Jarrell, who lived at **3916 Jenifer Street N.W.** at the time, offered to host Corso if he should ever find himself in Washington. Jarrell lived to regret that offer, because Gregory soon was on his doorstep, planning to stay indefinitely. Kerouac visited Corso at the Jarrells' and the two of them completely upset the household. Jack slept in Jarrell's basement while Corso took over the couch in the living room. In *Desolation Angels* Kerouac described the visit and how he raided the liquor cabinet and polished off half a bottle of Randalls' best Jack Daniels in one sitting. It didn't help matters when Corso decided to pound nails into the Jarrells' wall so that he could hang a picture he'd just painted of Michelangelo's David. After a few weeks Randall had to politely ask Gregory to leave and not return.

g. In 1966 **Allen Ginsberg** testified before a Senate Subcommittee on Drugs. A lifelong advocate for the decriminalization of drugs, Ginsberg also visited the offices of New York Senators Robert Kennedy and Jacob Javits to promote this cause. A few years later he returned to Washington to research allegations of CIA opium smuggling in Southeast Asia.

Allen Ginsberg testifying before the Senate

h. Over the years Washington institutions have hosted many poetry readings and lectures of Beat interest. In 1976, Allen Ginsberg and William S. Burroughs read together at the **Corcoran Gallery**. The **Folger Library** has featured readings by Lawrence Ferlinghetti, Denise Levertov, Allen Ginsberg, and many others. Perhaps the largest event took place at the **National Portrait Gallery** in April 1996, when the museum mounted a major exhibition called "Rebel Poets and Painters of the 1950s." The show opened with a mammoth reading by all the living Beats: Corso, Ferlinghetti, Ginsberg, McClure, and Jonathan Williams, who all read together for the last time.

i. On January 28, 2005, Lucien Carr died at the **George Washington University Hospital**. He had lived for more than a decade at **1844 Ontario Place N.W.** while working in Washington as the bureau chief for United Press International. In his obituary the *New York Times* called Carr the "Muse of the Beat Generation," and, indeed, although he never wrote anything himself, he inspired Kerouac, Burroughs, and Ginsberg.

j. In 1942, a young **David Amram** moved to Washington with his family and began classes at **Gordon Junior High School**. They lived in a small, sixteen-foot-wide house next to the Sheridan Garage at **2520 Q Street N.W.** Washington was still a segregated city in those days, and David remembered that the block he lived on was called a "checkerboard" because black and white families lived side by side.

k. From 1969 to 1970 **Nancy Peters** worked as a librarian at the **Library of Congress**. She found library work fascinating, but while on a vacation in San Francisco she was offered a job at City Lights. She grew to love the world of the independent publisher and before long had become Lawrence Ferlinghetti's partner in the business. Over the course of the next four decades she helped City Lights discover and publish a host of great books.

DELAWARE

1. New Castle. In 1960 **Jack Kerouac** rode with **Robert Frank** on one of the master photographer's picture-taking expeditions. The pair stopped at **Earl's Diner** on the **DuPont Highway, Route 40**, to grab a bite to eat. There, Robert Frank took a snapshot of a truck pulling a trailer stacked with new cars. Kerouac hadn't seen anything worth taking a picture of or writing about, but to the eye of Robert Frank everything was a worthy subject. Kerouac wrote about the trip in his article "On the Road to Florida," which was published posthumously in the 1970 issue of *Evergreen Review.* The actual diner was later moved to Somerville, Massachusetts, and renamed Kelly's Diner.

2. Newark. The **University of Delaware** is the largest institution in this otherwise small town. Some literary surprises are to be found in the **Morris Library**'s Department of Special Collections. Their holdings include the archives of Kay Boyle, Ishmael Reed, and Paul Bowles, whose papers were acquired shortly before the writer's death in Morocco in 1999. The library also has some fine examples of letters and manuscripts by Gregory Corso, Diane Di Prima, and John Wieners.

MARYLAND

1. Baltimore.

a. Poet **Frank O'Hara** was born in Baltimore on March 27, 1926. During his lifetime O'Hara gave his birth date as June 27, 1926, but he never realized that he was born in March, just six months after his parents were married. To avoid a scandal in their small town of Grafton, Massachusetts, they moved to Baltimore. He was born in Baltimore's **Maryland General Hospital** on **Linden Avenue**, and three months were added to his birth date so no one in the Irish Catholic family knew Frank was conceived out of wedlock. In addition to being one of the central figures of the New York School of poetry, he was also a close friend of many of the New York writers associated with the Beat Generation. Allen Ginsberg was a particular friend and dedicated a 1958 poem to O'Hara called "My Sad Self."

b. Composer **Philip Glass** was born in Baltimore on January 31, 1937. In the 1980s and 1990s Glass and Allen Ginsberg began to perform together at Buddhist benefit concerts. After Ginsberg's meditation teacher died in 1987, Glass introduced Allen to his own teacher, Gehlek Rinpoche. Allen liked Gehlek and respected his teaching method, so for the next ten years became a part of Gehlek's Jewel Heart sangha. Glass composed an opera, *Hydrogen Jukebox,* which was built around Ginsberg's words and put several other Ginsberg poems to music.

Philip Glass, Allen Ginsberg, and Gehlek Rinpoche

c. After getting lost somewhere along **U.S. Route 1** on one of their *On the Road* trips, **Neal Cassady** and **Jack Kerouac** reached the outskirts of Baltimore. There, Neal insisted that Jack take the wheel and make his way through the heavy rush-hour traffic for driving practice. It would have been okay, except that Neal and his wife LuAnne insisted on steering while Jack operated the pedals. Adding to the excitement, Neal turned up the radio volume to the maximum and beat on the dashboard of the Hudson Hornet as if it were a drum set. This was not the easiest way for Kerouac to improve his driving, and in fact, Jack never did get a driver's license.

d. In November 1977, **Allen Ginsberg** visited Baltimore with the young poet **Jonathan Robbins**. Robbins was convinced that Ginsberg was spending too much time being a literary showman instead of writing poetry and he wanted Allen to get back to the basics. Robbins planned that they would immerse themselves in classical literature, the works of Milton, Blake, and Poe in particular, during their two week visit to Baltimore. Out of this trip came Ginsberg's long poem "The Contest of Bards" with its song "The Rune," which he frequently sang at concerts.

2. Rockville. During World War II, **William Burroughs** was sent to **Chestnut Lodge, 500 West Montgomery**

131

Avenue, a psychiatric treatment center outside Washington, D.C., for a three-day evaluation. Burroughs had volunteered for military service, but what the army perceived as "mental problems" led to his honorable discharge in September 1942.

WEST VIRGINIA

1. Bethany. James Schuyler went to school at **Bethany College** just outside Wheeling. He is considered one of the major writers of the New York School, but he was also a close associate of many Beat writers. After his death in 1991 major collections of his poetry, art criticism, and diaries were published.

2. Charleston. Jack Kerouac passed through Charleston more than once, and in *On the Road* he mentioned that he "walked the hillbilly night of Charleston West Virginia" before moving on downriver through Kentucky and Ohio.

3. Wheeling. Jack Kerouac wrote about Wheeling in his book *Desolation Angels*. Near the end of that book, following a long cross-country trip with Allen Ginsberg and Peter Orlovsky, the trio arrived in Wheeling. Jack bought a quart of port wine and had what he called the "night of nights." They all got high and sang great Italian arias the rest of the way from Wheeling to Washington, D.C.

4. Weirton. The steel and coal mining town of Weirton made a vivid impression on **Jack Kerouac** when he passed through in 1949. In his journals he noted that it was "a mining town, haunted by scarred mountainsides beyond each sooty backstreet. Main Street was a beehive of shopping activity in the Friday afternoon. . . ."

VIRGINIA

1. Amherst. Sweet Briar College is located just outside the town of Amherst. In 1959 **Brenda Frazer** (later **Bonnie Bremser**) attended Sweet Briar for a brief period. If she hadn't met poet Ray Bremser in Washington, D.C., that year and fallen in love with him, she might have finished her degree at the college. But she took off with him to live what she thought would be a romantic life on the road. He introduced her to his world of poetry, and they indulged in more than their share of crime and drugs. She recorded her misadventures with Ray in *Troia: Mexican Memoirs*, 1969.

2. Arlington. In early 1942 **Jack Kerouac** worked on the construction of the Pentagon for a month and a half. He was not a hard worker and often would fall asleep on the job or walk off into the woods to write or just daydream. When Kerouac's foreman became aware of his prolonged absences, he was fired, ending his Arlington sojourn.

3. Fredericksburg. The University of Mary Washington, formerly the women's college of the University of Virginia, is located at **1301 College Avenue. Hettie Cohen** (later **Hettie Jones**) was seventeen when she attended classes here in 1951. As a dramatic arts and speech major she studied stagecraft, playwriting, and acting, and she wrote, directed, and performed in numerous productions. She had a show on the campus radio station, was an editor of the yearbook, published poems and essays in the school's literary magazine, and organized a traveling children's theater group which she took by bus to outlying communities. After graduating in 1955, she headed for Manhattan, where she met her future husband, LeRoi Jones. In 1992, the university inducted Hettie Jones into Phi Beta Kappa as a Distinguished Alumna.

4. Lexington. The **Virginia Military Institute** is located here in the picturesque Shenandoah Valley. It was in a class at VMI that the famous photograph of cadets reading *Howl* was taken by their professor, **Gordon Ball**. Ball had been the editor of several of Ginsberg's books and the manager of his Cherry Valley farm in the 1960s before he began his academic career. He invited Ginsberg to the campus several times, and Ginsberg's readings here were always popular. In *On the Road* **Jack Kerouac** mentions that he "heard the bird of Shenandoah and visited Stonewall Jackson's grave," which is also in Lexington.

"Cadets Read Howl" at V.M.I.

Photograph by Gordon Ball

NORTH CAROLINA

1. Asheville. In an early 1942 letter, Jack Kerouac was disappointed to write that although he was traveling in the south, "I never did hit Asheville, N.C., Wolfe's home town. I will next time." **Thomas Wolfe** had been a major influence not only on Kerouac, but on many novelists of the World War II era. Wolfe's family saga was the model for Jack's first book, *The Town and the City*. He was not alone among the Beats in his admiration for Wolfe either. Lawrence Ferlinghetti said that he attended the University of North Carolina in large part because that was the school with which Wolfe was associated. So significant was Wolfe to the nascent Beats that Allen Ginsberg described a pivotal all-night literary argument among Kerouac, Hal Chase, William Burroughs, and himself as "The Night of the Wolfeans." In his published journals, *The Book of Martyrdom and Artifice,* Ginsberg said that Jack and Hal were the Wolfeans, and he and William were what he termed "non-Wolfeans."

Asheville figures as prominently in Wolfe's books as Lowell does in Kerouac's. At **52 North Market Street** is the **Thomas Wolfe Memorial**. It was once a boardinghouse run by his mother, Julia Wolfe, and it was here that Wolfe lived between the ages 6 to 15. Wolfe called this house "Dixieland" in his autobiographical novel *Look Homeward, Angel*. Ironically, Wolfe's book was banned from Asheville's own public library for seven years following its publication because people believed it cast the local citizens in a bad light. "No man is a prophet in his own land" is an accurate proverb, as both Wolfe and Kerouac could attest. Both Asheville and Lowell have had love/hate relationships with their famous writer-sons. Wolfe died in Baltimore on September 15, 1938 and is buried in Asheville's **Riverside Cemetery** at **53 Birch Street**.

2. Chapel Hill.

a. In 1937 **Lawrence Ferlinghetti** enrolled in the School of Journalism at the **University of North Carolina**, in large part because his literary hero Thomas Wolfe had been a student there and had set part of his masterpiece, *Look Homeward, Angel*, in that town. Ferlinghetti described his own student days as "totally politically unconscious." He belonged to the **Kappa Sigma fraternity** and worked on the college newspaper, the *Daily Tar Heel,* where he was, among other things, a sports reporter. He was

Lawrence Ferlinghetti, 1941

Courtesy of the City Lights Archive

lucky to take a writing class from Phillips Russell, who introduced him to a wide range of authors. Ferlinghetti graduated with the class of 1941, just a few months before the attack upon Pearl Harbor. Like many other young men, he enlisted in the Navy and served for the duration of the war. Ferlinghetti has since returned to his alma mater to receive an honorary degree.

b. The **Wilson Library** in the center of the campus houses an impressive collection of Beat material, including the papers of Diane Di Prima, Edie Kerouac-Parker, and Henri Cru. The library also holds nearly complete collections of the publications of Lawrence Ferlinghetti, Allen Ginsberg, and the Grove Press.

3. Henderson. When Jack Kerouac's only sister, Nin, married Paul Blake, a North Carolina native, she moved to that state. Jack's mother Gabrielle lived with her from time to time, and Jack himself made several long visits to her various homes in North Carolina. When they were first married, Nin and Paul considered moving to the town of Henderson. Jack wrote to her, "the South enchants me anyway, but I don't know if I'd want to live there." He told her that he recalled passing through Henderson one night in a car and forever would remember the smell of honeysuckle perfuming the air.

4. Highlands. Highlands is at a tiny crossroads southwest of Asheville. Too small to appear on most maps, the community was nonetheless the home of **Jonathan Williams** and his Jargon Society Press from the early 1950s until Jonathan's death here on March 16, 2008. During those years Williams, who had been born in Asheville on March 8, 1929, published an astonishing number of postwar poets including many Beat and Black Mountain writers. The *New York Times* rightly called Jargon the "patron of the American imagination." Williams specialized in publishing intellectual works that other publishers too often ignored: *The Maximus Poems* by Olson, *Fables and Other Little Tales* by Patchen, and *All That Is Lovely in Men* by Creeley. In addition to these masterpieces, Williams issued books by Blackburn, Duncan, Eigner, McClure, Metcalf, Miller, Norse, Oppenheimer, Perkoff, Zukofsky, and dozens of other authors.

5. Kinston. In 1947, Jack Kerouac's sister and brother-in-law, **Nin and Paul Blake**, were living in Kinston when Jack and his mother visited them. Paul had recently been discharged from the army and was moving from place to place looking for employment. In early 1948 the Blakes left Kinston and moved to Rocky Mount, where both Jack and his mother visited often.

6. Lake Eden. Located near Asheville in the town of Lake Eden, **Black Mountain College** offered an alternative education to students from 1941 until it closed its doors in 1957. In its short life, the college attracted a remarkable roster of artists and writers interested in an avant-garde approach to education. The list of faculty instructors was impressive. John Cage taught here, as did Josef Albers, Merce Cunningham, Buckminster Fuller, Paul Goodman, and Robert Rauschenberg. Charles Olson taught at Black Mountain from 1948 until the college closed. His was the towering presence that drew a large number of writers and poets to study and teach here. Robert Creeley was Olson's student before he joined the faculty in 1954, and other students of Olson included John Wieners and Michael Rumaker. Ed Dorn was a member of the faculty for a while, and Robert Duncan was closely associated with the college.

7. Rocky Mount.

a. In *On the Road* **Jack Kerouac** disguised the exact location and people of Rocky Mount by renaming the town Testament, Virginia. The first time Kerouac saw Rocky Mount was in the 1940s, when his train made a layover here and he walked along the town's busy main street. In 1948, Jack's sister **Nin** and her husband **Paul Blake** moved here and found a little house at **1328 Tarboro Street** near the end of the road. In *On the Road,* Kerouac described his 1948 Christmas here when Neal Cassady, LuAnne Henderson, and Al Hinkle arrived from out of the blue in Neal's brand-new 1949 Hudson.

1328 Tarboro Street

Photograph by Bill Morgan

b. **Rocky Mount Train Station.** The handsome train and bus stations were close to each other when **Jack Kerouac** first came to town. During the forties and fifties these stations were central to his travels. **Neal Cassady** also visited Jack in Rocky Mount, and Jack wrote of him, "furiously he hustled into the railroad station" searching for cigarettes.

c. **Big Easonburg Woods, now West Mount.** The small frame house where **Nin and Paul Blake** lived during the mid-fifties is located about five miles south of Rocky Mount at **8230 West Mount Road**. **Jack Kerouac** describes this house in *The Dharma Bums*, and it was here that he wrote *Visions of Gerard* in 1955 while the rest of his family was away on a Christmas holiday. Jack sat at his typewriter in the kitchen and wrote the story of his older brother Gerard's childhood death. He visited the Blakes in this house many times

8230 West Mount Road

and asked that they put his rolltop desk filled with manuscripts on their screened-in back porch. He wrote, "They all wanted me to sleep on the couch in the parlor by the comfortable oil-burning stove but I insisted on making my room (as before) on the back porch with its six windows looking out on the winter barren cottonfield and the pine woods beyond, leaving all the windows open and stretching my good old sleeping bag on the couch there to sleep the pure sleep of winter nights. . . ." In Kerouac's day, the house was located on the spot where the adjacent Self-Serve convenience store now stands, but the house was moved when they constructed that store. At the time of Kerouac's stay, the house was in a rural area with a tall stand of pine trees in the back where he liked to walk and meditate. In order to be close to her daughter, Nin and Jack's mother Gabrielle moved into the house in September 1955.

d. 1311 Raleigh Road. At this address **Paul Blake** had his own TV repair shop. When he was in town, Kerouac would occasionally work for his brother-in-law delivering television sets for seventy-five cents an hour. Jack used the shop as his mailing address in the mid-fifties, probably because his mother had a habit of opening his letters. There are several other spots in the Rocky Mount area that Kerouac mentions in his books and letters. Once when his phlebitis acted up he had to spend a few days in the **Rocky Mount sanitarium**, and one summer Jack even worked at the **County Fair** directing cars in the parking lot.

e. Thelonious Sphere Monk was born in Rocky Mount on October 10, 1917. In the late fifties Allen Ginsberg met the great jazz pianist and gave him a copy of *Howl and Other Poems*. Later, when he asked Monk what he thought of it, Thelonious told Allen that he thought it "made sense," which delighted Ginsberg no end. Kerouac, Ginsberg, Kaufman, Joans, Lamantia, and many other writers during the 1940s and early 1950s were devoted to jazz in general and bebop like Monk's in particular. In fact, Kerouac's method of spontaneous writing was partially inspired by the riffs of musicians like Monk, Parker, Gillespie, Shearing, and Gaillard. It is not an exaggeration to say that without jazz there would have been no Beat Generation.

SOUTH CAROLINA

1. Camden. Gregory Corso's first great love affair was with **Elizabeth Hope Savage**, a native of Camden. When they met, she was a troubled seventeen-year-old girl eager to escape from the restrictions imposed on women by the moral code of mid-century America. Her father was mayor of Camden from 1948 to 1958, a founder of the local savings and loan, and active in local health care planning. Savage told Corso that as a teenager she had been placed in a mental hospital, where she underwent shock treatment. When Corso knew her in the mid-1950s, she was still living with her family in their beautiful home at **1919 Lyttleton Street**, and he visited her there, composing poetry and planning a novel. To Ginsberg Gregory wrote of Savage, "She is our Rimbaud." Over the years Sura (as Gregory called Hope) moved to India and lived a vagabond

Courtesy of the Allen Ginsberg Trust

Hope Savage and Gregory Corso

life there. In 1963 she met Allen Ginsberg on the streets of Calcutta and then disappeared again into the crowds. Corso never forgot her, and in fact an argument could be made that she was the one person that Gregory, always the romantic, truly loved.

2. Greenville. In *The Dharma Bums,* **Jack Kerouac** wrote about hitching a ride with a kindly naval officer who dropped him off in Greenville. In town, Jack walked for miles and said he got lost in the maze of downtown streets. When he passed a forge where some black men were laboring in the intense heat of the day, Jack felt he was "suddenly in hell again."

3. McClellanville. When **Jack Kerouac** visited the tiny town of McClellanville in 1960 with photographer **Robert Frank**, they found a "scene of beautiful old houses and incredible peace." Years later, Hurricane Hugo ended

141

all that, destroying many of the old homes in town and forcing businesses to move inland. Jack and Robert had stopped in town to document the great American road for *Life* magazine. Kerouac wrote about it in his essay "On the Road to Florida." There they found the old **Coast Barber Shop** run by 80-year-old Mr. Bryan. Frank took some wonderful pictures in the shop, and they also had their hair cut by the barber.

GEORGIA

1. Atlanta.

a. *The Great Speckled Bird* was Atlanta's countercultural newspaper during the late 1960s and early 1970s. Reporter Mike Wallace called the *Great Speckled Bird*, the *"Wall Street Journal* of the underground press." For a while, the *Bird* had offices at **204 Westminster Drive**, but in 1972 after publishing an article critical of Atlanta's mayor, it was fire bombed. They were part of the Liberation News Service, and as such published many Beat writers including Allen Ginsberg, Gary Snyder, Diane Di Prima, and Michael McClure.

b. In 2004, the **Woodruff Library** at **Emory University**, **201 Dowman Drive**, received a gift of what was believed to be the largest private collection of poetry books in the world. During his lifetime, Raymond Danowski amassed 60,000 volumes before generously donating them to the university. The vast collection contains many titles by Beat writers including a copy of Allen Ginsberg's mimeographed first publication of *Siesta in Xbalba*.

2. Gainesville. In *The Dharma Bums,* **Jack Kerouac** describes his arrival in Gainesville by bus. Unable to catch a ride out of town, he tried to sleep in the railroad yards but was chased out. Eventually he found a hotel room for $4 a night.

3. Savannah.

a. In 1960, on the road with **Robert Frank**, **Jack Kerouac** explored Savannah in the early morning hours. The pair happened upon a brand-new city garbage truck that was decorated with broken dolls' heads, flags, and horseshoes. Always looking for a great photo, Robert took some shots that appeared later in *Life* magazine. They also stopped at the bus station and both men captured more of the local color there, Robert with his camera and Jack with his pen. Kerouac described Frank as "the Dos Passos of American photographers" in his article "On the Road to Florida." It was published in *Evergreen Review* ten years later.

Robert Frank

b. In 1968 **Billy Burroughs Jr.,** the only son of William Burroughs, married his classmate, **Karen Beth Perry**, and the couple moved to her hometown, Savannah. While living here he wrote his autobiographical novel *Speed*, about the New York drug world he had recently been a part of.

FLORIDA

1. DeLand. In early 1981, **Billy Burroughs Jr.** was found unconscious in a ditch near Deland. He died shortly afterwards on March 3 in the **West Volusia Hospital** at **701 West Plymouth Avenue**. His death was a direct result of his inability to quit drinking even after a kidney transplant.

2. Jacksonville.

a. **Adelbert Lewis Marker** was originally from Jacksonville. He was a close friend of William S. Burroughs and was depicted as Eugene Allerton in the novel *Queer*. Marker met Burroughs when Marker was a student at Mexico City College in the early 1950s, and William became infatuated with the sexually ambivalent young man. For several months they explored Central and South America together searching for a drug called yage. On his way to Mexico around Christmas 1953, Allen Ginsberg stopped in Jacksonville to visit Marker. He was grateful when Marker generously loaned him a few dollars for his trip.

b. **Lawrence Ferlinghetti** married **Selden Kirby-Smith** in Jacksonville on April 10, 1951. He hadn't known Kirby when they were both graduate students at Columbia, but they met later in 1949 as passengers on a ship to France. In Paris they saw a lot of each other, and in 1951, after deciding to settle in San Francisco, Lawrence returned to Florida to marry her. Ivan Cousins, Ferlinghetti's Navy buddy and former roommate, was his only guest.

Lawrence Ferlinghetti and Selden Kirby-Smith

Courtesy of the City Lights Archive

3. Lake Geneva. In 1951, following his marriage to **Kirby**, **Lawrence Ferlinghetti** and his bride honeymooned in this small inland town where Kirby's mother owned a cabin on Lake

Geneva. After the honeymoon they set up housekeeping in San Francisco.

4. Miami.

a. In 1969, **Allen Ginsberg** was invited to read at the **Marine Stadium** on the **Virginia Key** with his father, poet **Louis Ginsberg**. While Allen was reading his poetry, the police turned off the microphone in order to silence his sexual references and antiwar statements. Ginsberg challenged that censorship in court, and the judge allowed him to resume his reading a week later. In 1972, Ginsberg returned to Miami's Marine Stadium with Peter Orlovsky to demonstrate at the Republican National Convention where Richard Nixon was easily nominated for a second term in spite of mounting protests against his Vietnam policy. In 1992, after Hurricane Andrew devastated the region, the stadium was condemned.

b. In the early 1950s **Gregory Corso** lost all of his poetry manuscripts at the **Greyhound Bus Terminal** in Miami. The package contained his earliest poems, written while serving time in prison in upstate New York.

5. Orange City. Billy Burroughs Jr. was sent to the **Green Valley School** near Orange City to continue drug rehabilitation after his release from the Lexington Narcotics Hospital in Kentucky. He wrote about this period in his autobiographical novel *Kentucky Ham*. Green Valley was a private institution run by an eccentric minister named Reverend Von Hilsheimer. While at Green Valley, Billy met seventeen-year-old Georgia native Karen Perry, whom he married in 1968. While Billy wrote, Karen worked as a waitress, but their marriage was short-lived.

6. Orlando. Jack Kerouac made his home in Orlando during the pre-Disneyworld 1950s and early 1960s. In

order to find work, Paul Blake and his wife, Kerouac's sister Nin, moved to Orlando from North Carolina. In late 1956 Jack's mother, Gabrielle, came to stay with the Blakes at **1219 Yates Street**, and Jack visited them frequently. On his first trip he was thrilled to find his old rolltop desk filled with manuscripts already sitting on their screened-in back porch. It was from their Yates Street house that Kerouac left on his trip to visit William Burroughs in Tangiers early in 1957. On May 6 of the same year, after his return from Morocco, Jack and his mother moved briefly to Berkeley, California.

By July 1957 Jack and his mother had tired of California and moved back to Orlando. Kerouac rented a house at **1418½ Clouser Avenue** and lived here until April 1958. It was here that he wrote *The Dharma Bums*. He was still living here in October 1957 when he went to New York for the publication of *On the Road*. In the city he stayed with his girlfriend, Joyce Johnson, for a few weeks, and together they read the first laudatory *New York Times* review that made his book a bestseller. Then in 1958, flush with the initial success of his novel, Jack left the Clouser Avenue home and bought a house in Northport, New York. The Orlando house is now owned by an organization known as the Kerouac Project, which often hosts guest writers here.

Kerouac could never find a place that was just right for him and his mother, and by the spring of 1961 they were back in Orlando again. This time they bought a house at **1309 Alfred Drive**, **Kingswood Manor**, once again to be close to Nin. The ranch-style house was air-conditioned and surrounded by a six-foot-tall fence to keep out unwanted visitors. In that house Kerouac finished writing *Big Sur*, the novel in which he describes his own alcoholic breakdown. The Kerouacs remained in that house from May 1961 until December 1962.

On September 19, 1964, Nin died suddenly of a heart

attack in Orlando. By that time she and her husband had separated, and, left with no money, she had had been forced to sell most of her furniture. She moved to the College Park section of Orlando in the **14th Fairway Apartments**, so-called because of the Dubsdread Golf Course just across the street at **549 West Par Street**. Nin was buried in Orlando's **Greenwood Cemetery**, and when her estranged husband Paul Blake Sr. died in 1972, his ashes were placed in an unmarked grave near her own.

7. Palm Beach. In 1951, not long after William Burroughs accidentally shot and killed his wife, their son, **Billy Burroughs**, was sent to live with William's parents in St. Louis. In the spring of 1952, the elder Burroughses moved to Palm Beach and bought a comfortable house at **202 Sanford Avenue**, a palm tree–lined street. Before long they opened an antique store named **Cobblestone Gardens** at **233 Phipps Plaza**, but soon relocated it to **327 Worth Avenue**. In December 1952, William skipped bail in Mexico City and, fearing a long prison sentence, decided not to return for his trial. Every year or so William visited his parents and his son in Palm Beach, but he never stayed very long. Late in 1953, Allen Ginsberg stopped to visit the Burroughs family on his own way to Mexico. They generously took him out to dinner and paid for his hotel room that night. William's father, Mortimer Burroughs, died in Palm Beach on January 19, 1965, and his wife Laura continued to care for Billy as best she could until her death in 1970.

8. St. Petersburg.

a. In September 1964, **Jack Kerouac** and his mother moved from Northport, Long Island, to a house at **5155 Tenth Avenue North** in St. Petersburg. There Kerouac spent a good deal of his time drinking at places like **The Wild Boar**, a local hangout. During this period Jack made a trip to Paris in search of his lost ancestors. The story of that drunken fiasco is related in the short book *Satori in Paris*, which Jack wrote in this house in August 1965. After Nin's death, Gabrielle asked to return north, so Jack agreed and found a house for them in Hyannis, Massachusetts.

Moving yet again from Hyannis to Lowell after his mother had a stroke, Jack and his new wife, Stella Sampas, returned with Gabrielle to St. Petersburg in September 1968. They bought the house at **5169 Tenth Avenue North**, right next to the one they had owned a few years earlier. Jack had only a year to enjoy his new life there with Stella. One night in October 1969 he began to hemorrhage and spit up blood. He was rushed to **St. Anthony's Hospital** at **1200 Seventh Avenue North,** where he passed away on October 21, 1969, at 5:15 in the morning. The medical report listed the cause of death as "gastrointestinal hemorrhage, bleeding gastric varix from cirrhosis of the liver, excessive ethanol intake." In short, he drank himself to death.

Kerouac was laid in an open casket at the **Rhodes Funeral Home, 635 Fourth Street North,** and his mother was brought to see him in a wheelchair. Stella and Jack's mother continued to live in the house until Gabrielle died of a stroke in 1973 at the age of 88 having outlived all three of her children.

Jack Kerouac obituary

b. Another Beat figure, **David Amram**, also lived in St. Petersburg. In 1936, when David was six, the Amram family moved to **Pass-a-Grille Beach**, where they lived for a year in a ramshackle bungalow with a screened-in porch. They had moved here from Pennsylvania because David's sister was in poor health and needed to recuperate in a warmer climate.

9. Sarasota. In May 1951 **Lew Welch** moved to Sarasota, where he shared a house with Peter Oser and five other young men, all students of scientology. Welch later wrote in a letter that this was his "Walden in Florida" period. When they weren't studying, Lew and his housemates spent a good deal of time fishing. In the fall Welch left to attend classes at the University of Chicago.

KENTUCKY

1. Ashland. During his final bus trip in *On the Road*, **Jack Kerouac** describes passing through Ashland, where he saw "a lonely girl under the marquee of a closed up show." Quite possibly it was the landmark **Paramount Theater** at **1300 Winchester Avenue**.

2. Lexington. The Lexington Narcotic Farm, actually named the **U.S. Public Health Service Hospital**, was the first hospital founded in this country for the treatment of patients addicted to habit-forming drugs. From the time it opened in 1935 until it closed in 1974, thousands of people came here to break their addictions. In

January 1948, **William Burroughs** spent two weeks here during one of his first attempts to kick a drug habit. In *Junky* Burroughs describes some of his experiences at Lexington, which he said was run like a minimum-security prison complete with a working farm and dairy. Nearly twenty

years later his son, **Billy Burroughs Jr.**, was sent to Lexington for treatment, and he also wrote about his "cure" in his own book, *Kentucky Ham.*

3. Louisville. Hunter S. Thompson was born in Louisville on July 18, 1937. His parents were Jack Robert and Virginia Davidson Ray Thompson. After living in a series of rental homes, they bought a bungalow at **2437 Ransdell Avenue** in a suburban area known as the Highlands, a part of the well-to-do Cherokee Triangle neighborhood. Thompson's father died in July 1952 just before Hunter's fifteenth birthday, and after his death Hunter's mother became a heavy drinker, something that her son couldn't tolerate. Although Hunter joined the Castlewood Athletic Club and excelled in sports, he was constantly in trouble. He attended the **I. N. Bloom Elementary School** at **1627 Lucia Avenue** before going on to **Atherton High School, 3000 Dundee Road**. In 1952, soon after the death of his father, he began attending **Louisville Male High School, 4409 Preston Highway**. Later Thompson spent a month in the **Jefferson County Jail** on **Court Place** after being arrested as an accessory to robbery. After his release he joined the Air Force and left Louisville.

TENNESSEE

1. Nashville.

a. **Carolyn Robinson** (later **Carolyn Cassady**) moved to Nashville with her family when she was eight years old. In 1931 her father had been hired as a professor of biochemistry at the **Vanderbilt University School of Medicine**. She graduated from high school at the **Ward-Belmont Preparatory School for Girls** in Nashville. Years later, in 1950, the school was sold and the buildings became part of Belmont College.

Although Carolyn enjoyed her school, she disliked Nashville and spent her summer vacations at Glen Lake in Michigan. She described their 1823 Nashville house as having the faded splendor of a Southern plantation mansion, complete with old slave cabins. It was named **Ravenswood** in honor of Sam Houston, whose nickname was "The Raven." The house is now used as a conference center.

b. In 1958, **John Montgomery**, whom Jack Kerouac calls Henry Morley in *The Dharma Bums*, earned his master's degree in library science at **Peabody College**, part of **Vanderbilt University**. Montgomery was one of the first scholars of the Beat Generation and published books at his Fels and Firn Press.

MISSISSIPPI

Courtesy of the Allen Ginsberg Trust

Philip Whalen

1. Biloxi. Philip Whalen went through two months of basic training at **Keesler Field** in Biloxi after he was drafted into the Army Air Corps in 1943. The base had been established in 1941 to support the troop buildup for World War II; it was here that recruits were trained in aircraft mechanics and maintenance. During the period that Whalen was at Keesler, the base also trained the Tuskegee Airmen, an elite African American unit.

2. Jackson. Gordon Ball, Allen Ginsberg's editor and friend, lived at **2900 Downing Street** in Jackson while he was teaching at Tougaloo College. Ginsberg visited him several times during the 1980s to work on various books, and while in town he gave readings at the college.

3. Oxford. In April 1987, **Allen Ginsberg** decided to take his stepmother, Edith Ginsberg, and his old friend, the musicologist **Harry Smith**, on a tour of the Mississippi River Delta. This gave Ginsberg a chance to spend time with Edith and gave Smith a chance to visit the blues country that had produced so much of the music that he collected in the seminal recordings *The Anthology of American Folk Music.* They visited **"Ole Miss"** and toured the **Southern Folklore Center Blues Archive** before going on to Clarksdale and Holly Springs.

ALABAMA

1. Citronelle. William Seward Burroughs, the paternal grandfather of the writer William S. Burroughs, died in Citronelle in 1898. The elder Burroughs was an inventor, best known for perfecting the adding machine. By the late 1800s, Citronelle had become a health resort due to the mild climate, local herbs (like the citronella plant, from which the town derived its name), and healing waters. Grandfather Burroughs, who suffered from chronic bad health all his life and died at the age of 43, was probably in town to partake of those cures. Some people thought that Burroughs was wealthy because of his famous grandfather, but he was always quick to point out that he inherited very little of the Burroughs Corporation money.

2. Mobile. In *On the Road* **Jack Kerouac** describes his trip with **Neal Cassady, LuAnne Henderson**, and **Al Hinkle** through Mobile on their way to visit William S. Burroughs in New Orleans. "Rolling into Mobile over the long tidal highway we all took our winter clothes off and enjoyed the southern temperature," Jack wrote. When they came upon a wreck blocking the road just beyond town, Cassady swerved the Hudson Hornet he was driving through a gas station at 70 mph and back onto the road without slowing down. All of this must have been along **US 90**, which was a major east-west highway at the time.

3. Monroeville. Although born in New Orleans on September 30, 1924, **Truman Capote** spent most of his early childhood in a small house two blocks south of the town square, on **South Alabama Avenue**. His next-door neighbor was **Harper Lee**, who became a lifelong friend. Later, Harper helped Truman with the research for his book *In Cold Blood* while working on her own *To Kill a Mockingbird*. Capote will be forever linked with the Beats by an insulting quip he made about Kerouac on David Susskind's TV show "Open End." "It isn't writing at all, it's typing," Capote said of *On the Road*. The Capote house burned to the ground in 1940, and a second house built on the same site was demolished in 1988. A fragment of the stone wall from the original house still exists near the town's Truman Capote historic marker.

4. Tuscaloosa. **Timothy Leary** was a student at the **University of Alabama** on two occasions. In 1942, after being dismissed from West Point, Leary enrolled at Tuscaloosa, where he became interested in psychology. Leary was expelled after he spent the night with his girlfriend in **Tutwiler Hall**, the women's dorm. Without a student deferment he was in a precarious position, so he enrolled immediately in the University of Illinois. In spite of that he was drafted in January 1943 and ordered to report for basic training at Fort Eustis, Virginia. Following his military service he was reinstated at the University of Alabama and finished his requirements for a bachelor of arts degree on August 23, 1945, via correspondence courses, without ever returning to Tuscaloosa.

William S. Burroughs, 1961

VI. West South Central States

LOUISIANA

1. Algiers. Looking out over the river from the deck of the New-Orleans-to-Algiers ferry, Jack Kerouac caught his first glimpse of the town where **William S. Burroughs** lived from June 1948 to April 1949. "Old sleepy Algiers with its warped woodsides," Jack wrote in *On the Road*. Jack,

Burroughs House historic marker

Neal Cassady, LuAnne Henderson, and Al Hinkle arrived to pick up Al's wife Helen, who had been impatiently waiting for the them to drive her back west. William, his common-law wife Joan, and their children Julie and Billy lived in a typical "shotgun-style" house at **509 Wagner Street**. Joan Burroughs had a drug habit by this time and was ingesting three inhaler strips of benzedrine every day. Kerouac wrote, "Her face, once plump and Germanic and pretty, had become stony and red and gaunt." Burroughs himself was hooked on morphine at the time, so they were both strung out. William wrote about this period of his life in *Junky*. While staying with Burroughs, Jack and Neal visited the bookie joints in Gretna, the next town up the river. In 1996 a historic marker was placed in front of the Wagner Street house to commemorate Burroughs's residence.

2. Baton Rouge. Andrei Codrescu was appointed MacCurdy Distinguished Professor of English at **Louisiana State University** in Baton Rouge. As a boy growing up in Romania, reading the books of Beat writers in Romanian translation, he could never have imagined that he would end up teaching their work deep in the American South. In 1966, at the age of twenty, he emigrated and became friends with many of those same writers. Once in the United States Andrei began to publish an influential literary journal titled *Exquisite Corpse* and became the poetry columnist for National Public Radio.

3. New Orleans.

a. When **William S. Burroughs** first moved to Louisiana in the late spring of 1948, he found a house at **111 Transcontinental Drive** in New Orleans, but he didn't stay there long. He moved across the river to the quieter village of Algiers, accessible only by ferry in those days, before the Greater New Orleans and CCC Bridges were built. Although Burroughs explored the queer scene in the French Quarter, it wasn't for him.

509 Wagner Street, Algiers

He was repelled by the flamboyant Southern queens he found there. In *Junky* he described this period in detail.

After Burroughs had lived in Algiers for a year, his father signed a contract to buy a house for his son and family at **1128-30 Burgundy** in the French Quarter, but they never had a chance to live there. One day in early April 1949, Burroughs was arrested while trying to score drugs on **Lee Circle**. He was sent to the **Touro Infirmary** for treatment. Before his case came to trial that October, Burroughs fled to Mexico City, and later his father sold the house.

b. In his book *Desolation Angels* **Jack Kerouac** describes his layover in New Orleans when he and his mother were taking the bus to the West Coast. His mother spoke French fluently, so she enjoyed talking with the locals as they bought souvenirs for Jack's sister. Even though they liked the city, they knew that New Orleans was too expensive for them.

c. Poet **Bob Kaufman**, most often associated with San Francisco's North Beach, was born in New Orleans on April 18, 1925. Kaufman, the son of a German

Jewish father and a Roman Catholic Black mother from Martinique, was one of fourteen children. He said that his grandmother introduced him to voodoo rituals and New Orleans jazz, both of which became a significant influence on his poetry. At age thirteen, Kaufman ran away to join the Merchant Marine.

Bob Kaufman, early 1980s

Courtesy of the City Lights Archive

4. Opelousas. In *On the Road,* **Jack Kerouac** describes

the time he and **Neal Cassady** crossed the country and stopped in Opelousas. Since Neal had not been able to con William Burroughs out of any money for their trip, they were nearly broke. Neal stopped the car for gas and oil, and Jack walked down the street to a grocery store to buy bread and cheese. Inside the little store, the owners were eating in the back and didn't hear Jack enter, so he slipped out the door with his groceries. In the meantime, Neal had stolen a carton of cigarettes from the gas station, and so they headed on, without giving much thought to the people they had robbed.

5. Starks. After leaving William Burroughs in New Orleans, **Jack Kerouac** and **Neal Cassady** took **Route 190** through Starks. Kerouac wrote in *On the Road* that they saw a "great red glow in the sky" which they knew could have been anything from a fish fry to a forest fire, but as usual they did not take time to stop to investigate.

ARKANSAS

1. Fayetteville. John Clellon Holmes, author of *Go*, the first published Beat novel, was on the faculty at the **University of Arkansas** for many years. He began lecturing at the university in 1957 and, in 1966, became the school's first writer in residence. While teaching here, Holmes lived  at **601 Park Avenue**. Although he always maintained a home in Connecticut, he began teaching full time in the fall of 1975 and served as a full professor from 1980 until his retirement in 1986. The year after Holmes left teaching he died of throat cancer at age sixty-one. The University of Arkansas Press published three collections of his essays and a book of his poems after his death.

2. Hot Springs. In early November 1994, **Allen Ginsberg** appeared at the Hot Springs Documentary Film Festival at the request of Jerry Aronson, whose movie *The Life and Times of Allen Ginsberg* was being featured. Ginsberg stayed at the grand old **Arlington Hotel** at **239 Central Avenue** and gave a performance of his poetry during his visit there. After hearing many people ending their sentences with the dialect phrase "ya hear," Ginsberg penned a poem that began "The world is an empty dream, ya hear / They say the sun's not eternal, got four billion years to go . . ."

3. Mena. When **Kenneth Patchen** was eighteen he attended Alexander Meiklejohn's Experimental College at the University of Wisconsin. The next year, 1939, Meiklejohn moved to **Commonwealth College** in Mena and Patchen followed him to that short-lived but radical labor college founded on the theories of Eugene Debs. After a semester Kenneth grew disenchanted with the academic world and began to wander the country as a vagabond.

4. Salem. **Joe Brainard** was born in Salem, Arkansas, on March 11, 1942, even though he always told everyone that he was from Tulsa. In 1943, as a baby, he moved with his family to Oklahoma where he grew up not really having much memory of Salem. As a boy in Tulsa he showed early artistic talent and won several local art contests. Later he moved to New York City and illustrated the books of many of his friends who were associated with the St. Mark's Poetry Project. Poets Ted Berrigan, Kenward Elmslie, Dick Gallup, Ron Padgett, and Anne Waldman were among his closest friends until his death in 1994.

OKLAHOMA

1. Tulsa. A group of friends who became prominent members of the New York School of poets spent their early years together in Tulsa. **Ted Berrigan** earned both his bachelor's and master's degrees from **Tulsa University** at **800 South Tucker Drive**. When the university sent Ted's M.A. diploma to him, he returned it with a note that read, "Dear Sirs: I am the master of no art." Ted was living in a rented room not far from campus when he became friends with two younger poets who had been raised in Tulsa, **Ron Padgett** and **Dick Gallup**. In 1959–1960, while they were in **Central High School**, they edited the little magazine *White Dove Review*. Another Tulsa friend, **Joe Brainard**, was their art director and lived with his family at **159 North Columbia Place**. Like Padgett, Brainard went to **Whittier Elementary** and **Cleveland Junior High**. Years later they all ended up in the same neighborhood on New York's Lower East Side. Ron Padgett wrote about their favorite all-night hangout, **Earl's Cafe** on **East 11th Street**, a block east of Harvard in Tulsa. "For a nickel you could sit there with your coffee and get endless refills from the waitress." Tulsa is a recurrent theme in their work, and Padgett wrote books with titles like *Tulsa Kid* and *Oklahoma Tough: My Father, King of the Tulsa Bootleggers.*

Left to right: Ron Padgett, Dick Gallup, Michael Marsh, Joe Brainard, Central High School, Tulsa, OK

TEXAS

1. Abilene. In *On the Road* **Jack Kerouac** described crossing Texas from north to south, as he and Neal Cassady did on their way to Mexico. In Abilene, a town "where they shipped the cows and shot it up for gumshoes and drank red-eye," they stopped for lunch on the highway just south of town.

2. Alvarado. Terry Southern, the author of *Red-Dirt Marijuana* and *Flash and Filigree,* was born in Alvarado on May 1, 1924. Southern began to write satire when he was only eleven or twelve years old, and as a boy he re-wrote Edgar Allan Poe stories because "they didn't go far enough." Terry, the son of a pharmacist, went to high school in Dallas before going on to Southern Methodist University and the University of Chicago.

3. Amarillo. When **Jack Kerouac** and **Neal Cassady** drove through Amarillo, Jack felt nostalgic about the buffalo tents that he believed might have been pitched there only a few decades earlier. In *On the Road* he complained that those days were gone forever, replaced by gas stations and "new 1950 jukeboxes with immense ornate snouts and ten-cent slots and awful songs."

4. Austin. One of America's greatest treasuries of Beat Literature is the **Harry Ransom Humanities Research Center at the University of Texas at Austin**. In the library building at **21st and Guadalupe** are Kerouac's *On the Road* notebooks, his correspondence with Allen Ginsberg, and many other Beat artifacts. The HRC now has a large gallery area with a wide variety of changing exhibits of everything from the Gutenberg Bible to the *On the Road* scroll, which was displayed here in 2008.

5. Beaumont. Jack Kerouac, Neal Cassady, and LuAnne Henderson were getting tired of traveling when they finally hit the state line near Beaumont. "Texas! It's Texas! Beaumont oiltown!" they shouted. There the "huge oil tanks and refineries loomed like cities in the oily fragrant air," Kerouac wrote in *On the Road*.

6. Beeville. In May 1948, **William S. Burroughs** and **Joan Vollmer** were caught having sex in their parked car just outside Beeville. Burroughs was arrested and fined $173, then had to be bailed out by his parents after spending a night in the local jail. In a letter Burroughs wrote, "I lost my Texas driving license for driving while drunk and public indecency." The two were caught by legendary no-nonsense Texas lawman Vail Ennis, one of the toughest cops in the state.

Beeville courthouse

7. Brownsville. Heading back to North Carolina from Mexico City in July 1952 **Jack Kerouac** crossed the border at Brownsville. The first man who gave him a ride was Hotrod Johnny Bowen, who insisted that Jack.with him on an all-night binge. They hit all the local dives in town. In the town of Harlingen, a Mexican medical student gave Jack a ride north on Highway 77 to Rosenberg, a town near Houston, and from there he slowly made his way back home.

8. Clint. As **Neal Cassady** drove **Jack Kerouac** and **LuAnne Henderson** through Texas, he complained to them that no matter where they were in the West, they could hear the Clint radio station. His beef with the station was that they did nothing but play commercials for a correspondence school. Neal had listened to it from various reformatories and prisons in which he had done time, and sure enough, as they passed through Clint, they saw the incredibly tall antenna tower of the radio station looming over some old shacks.

9. Conroe. While living on their decrepit farm in New Waverly, **William Burroughs** and **Joan Vollmer**, his common-law wife, had a son named Billy. He was born in a hospital in Conroe, the closest medical center to New Waverly. On July 21, 1947, Joan gave birth easily, so the next day they drove back to the farm with the baby in their jeep.

10. Deweyville. On one of the cross-country drives with **Neal Cassady** that **Jack Kerouac** describes in *On the Road*, Jack wrote, "The country turned strange and dark near Deweyville. Suddenly we were in the swamps." He fantasized about finding a secluded jazz joint hidden in the marshland and all the mysterious adventures they would have there. But, as usual, they were in too much of a hurry to stop and they kept on "high-balling" along the road.

11. Dilley. In the final passage of *On the Road*, **Jack Kerouac** writes about finding himself standing alone on the hot summer road under a street light in Dilley, Texas. He heard footsteps in the dark and a tall white-haired old man clomped past him with a backpack. He uttered the phrase, "Go moan for man." Its exact meaning was a mystery to Jack, but he thought about it philosophically and used the phrase in the book as if it were a command from another world.

12. El Paso. It wasn't unusual for **Neal Cassady, Jack Kerouac,** and **LuAnne Henderson** to run out of money on their trips. Once, when they pulled into the El Paso bus station, they tried unsuccessfully to hustle a few dollars. Neal suggested that they mug someone, but that was not for Jack. Cassady wandered off on his own for a little while and came back with the needed money. No one ever asked him where it came from.

13. Galveston. Late in August 1951, **Allen Ginsberg** and **Lucien Carr** drove from New York to Mexico City to visit William and Joan Burroughs. When they got there, they found that William was out of town, but they were able to spend a few days driving wildly around Mexico with Joan and her two children. On the way back to New York their car broke down and Ginsberg stayed in a Galveston hotel to wait for the repairs while Carr flew back to his job. On September 7, Allen opened the Galveston newspaper and was shocked to read that Burroughs had returned to Mexico City and shot and killed Joan during a drunken game of William Tell. A few years later, Ginsberg wrote the poem "Dream Record," which describes his dream about visiting Joan's grave.

14. Houston. In 1947 while William S. Burroughs was living on a farm in New Waverly with Joan and their two children, Herbert Huncke came to help with the chores. With his street smarts he was immediately able to find a drug connection in Houston and as a result they often made the trip in Burroughs's jeep to restock their shelves with drugs, alcohol, and other necessities. In August, while Ginsberg and Cassady were visiting the farm, they made a trip to Houston with Huncke and stayed at the **Brazos Hotel, 608 Preston Street**, near the Southern Pacific train station. Neal picked up a woman and brought her back to the room, which disappointed Allen, since he was hoping to spend the night in bed with Neal. Huncke wanted to find male companionship, so he was angry as well. Hoping to escape all this angst, Ginsberg decided to ship out and leave his troubles behind. He signed on to the S. S. *John Blair* at the **Freeport Coal Docks** and set sail for Africa on September 6.

15. Huntsville. After he graduated from Harvard, William Burroughs's best friend **Kells Elvins** found a job in Huntsville as a psychologist at the state prison. There he worked on his unfinished master's thesis, "Forty-Four Incestuous Fathers of Texas." In 1938 Burroughs visited Elvins in Huntsville for a few weeks, during which time they made plans to go into the ranching business together in southern Texas.

16. Laredo.

a. Laredo was the quintessential seedy border town when **Jack Kerouac** passed through on his trips to and from Mexico. "It was the bottom and dregs of America where all the heavy villains sink," he wrote in *On the Road.* Jack always seemed to become philosophical as he either left or entered the country. He mentioned that it was 767 miles from that point to Mexico City, and so crossing the border represented either a new beginning or an end to some adventure.

b. Laredo was also the town where **Timothy Leary** was picked up crossing the border on December 22, 1965, and charged with the possession of a small amount of marijuana. Leary's eighteen-year-old daughter Susan had hidden the grass in her pants, but to avoid problems for her he accepted the fine of $30,000 and thirty years in prison. This marked the beginning of serious legal difficulties for Tim. It was an eerie reminder of the line from Ginsberg's "Howl," written ten years earlier: "who got busted in their pubic beards returning through Laredo with a belt of marijuana for New York."

17. McAllen. When William Burroughs's oldest friend, **Kells Elvins,** died in New York on February 5, 1962, his body was sent to McAllen for burial. Burroughs was in Europe at the time and didn't hear about his death until months later, when he tried to contact Kells through his mother. The cemetery is not far from Pharr, where he and Burroughs had tried their hands at farming a decade earlier.

Kells Elvins's grave

18. New Waverly. Late in 1946 **William Burroughs** bought a ninety-seven-acre farm on the edge of the bayou about twelve miles outside the sleepy crossroads town of New Waverly. Its isolated location in the middle of nowhere appealed to Burroughs—he believed that he would be able to grow marijuana and opium poppies without any interference from the law. To help work the dilapidated farm, he and Joan Vollmer invited Herbert Huncke to bring some marijuana seeds down from New York City. Joan was pregnant with William's son, Billy. A month after the baby was born Neal Cassady and Allen Ginsberg came to visit. That fall, when the marijuana was harvested, Cassady drove it to New York to sell, but it wasn't cured properly and rotted in Mason jars before he was able to sell it.

New Waverly City Hall

19. Odessa. On March 30, 2005, Robert Creeley died of pneumonia and complications from lung disease in a hospital in Odessa. That winter, he had been the writer in residence for the Lannan Foundation in Marfa, Texas.

20. Ozona. While driving through Texas, **Neal Cassady** stopped in the sage desert near Ozona and stripped off all his clothes. He ran naked along the road "yippiing and leaping," Kerouac wrote in *On the Road*. Then he encouraged Jack and LuAnne Henderson to do the same thing. They all rode through the hot afternoon naked, occasionally passing a truck driver who would swerve when he looked down from his cab.

21. Pharr. In June 1946, **William Burroughs** visited **Kells Elvins**, who was living on a farm along **Route 1** in Pharr. Burroughs thought he would buy farmland of his own, grow citrus fruit, and make a fortune without having to do any work, but the easy success he hoped for never quite panned out. William made some investments in agricultural property around Pharr, but didn't buy a home right away. He, Joan Vollmer, and her daughter Julie stayed in a cheap motel in nearby McAllen while William organized things. Then in the summer of 1949, the family moved into a ranch-style house just behind Elvins's orange groves, now the site of a shopping center. Joan was using a tremendous amount of benzedrine, and Burroughs frequently visited the San Juan drugstores to replenish her supply of inhalers. In his backyard, Burroughs built an orgone accumulator, an invention that was designed to trap the energy of the cosmos. Soon they bought their own fifty-acre farm in Edinburg at the corner of **Monte Cristo and Cesar Chavez** (formerly **Morningside Drive**) where he grew carrots, peas, lettuce, and cotton. Rob Johnson has done thorough research on Burroughs's activities in south Texas, and his book *The Lost Years of*

William S. Burroughs: Beats in South Texas is a treasure trove of information on the places that Burroughs knew and frequented here.

22. San Antonio. In *On the Road,* **Jack Kerouac** tells the story of taking Stan Shepard (in real life, Frank Jeffries, a Denver friend of Neal Cassady's) with them to Mexico City, where Neal was planning to get a Mexican divorce from Diana Hansen. Jeffries had been stung by an insect as they were leaving Denver, and his arm was infected by the time that got to San Antonio. They stopped at a downtown clinic and Frank received a shot of penicillin while Jack and Neal wandered around "digging everything," even the air itself. Jack wrote, "It was fragrant and soft—the softest air I'd ever known. . . ."

WEST
REGION

Neal Cassady

VII. Mountain States

COLORADO

1. Denver. There are a handful of towns in the country that are essential destinations for anyone interested in retracing the footsteps of the Beats. Denver is one of those towns. Neal and Carolyn Cassady, Jack Kerouac, and Allen Ginsberg all spent eventful days in Denver, and it was seminal to the development of the Beat Generation.

a. First and foremost, Denver was **Neal Cassady**'s town. He literally grew up on the streets here. In 1928, when Neal was two years old, his family moved to **23rd Street between Welton Street and Glenarm Place** from Salt Lake City. There they lived in back of a two-chair barbershop where Neal Sr. worked. The earliest known address for the Cassady family is from November 1932 when they lived in the **Snowden apartment building** at **2563 Champa Street**. Other documents give the address of the same building as **910 26th Street**, since it occupied a corner lot with an entrance on each street.

However, in 1933 a school official noted that the "family is unknown at this [Champa Street] address." In his autobiography, *The First Third*, Neal Cassady said that his father worked in a barber shop in that same building and described it as a "sad little shop so filled with contention." The Cassadys also lived in the **Kingston Row townhouses** at **411 21st Street** and later at **407 21st Street**.

When Cassady was six, his parents separated, and when he was ten his mother died. Neal was left to grow up with his alcoholic father in various flophouses around town. During the early years when both parents were still alive Neal spent the school year with his mother and traveled with his father during the summers. For a while Neal's father lived in the faded elegance of the **Metropolitan Hotel** on the corner of **Market and 16th Street**, but he couldn't always afford anything that comfortable. At other times he had a cheap room in the **Rossonian Hotel** and hung out in the pool halls along the Larimer Street skid row district. That area has been obliterated by urban renewal, and today there are few signs of the breakfast missions and soup kitchens that Neal frequented.

Neal Cassady at his job parking cars

Courtesy of the Allen Ginsberg Trust

Neal's mother, who died in the **Denver General Hospital** on May 23, 1936, was buried in **Mount Olivet Cemetery** at **12801 West 44th Avenue** in Wheat Ridge. When Neal Cassady Sr. passed away, he was also buried in Mount Olivet Cemetery in an unmarked grave.

It wasn't until July 23, 1938, two years after his mother died, that Neal was baptized a Catholic at **Holy Ghost Church, 1900 California Street**. The following year he gave his address as **2519 Tremont** on a school document. Although Catholic, Neal attended public school in Denver. After starting at **Colfax Elementary School** in September 1931, he continued at **Ebert Grammar School** in 1932 and went on to **Cole Junior High School** in 1938. By the time he entered **East High School** in January 1942, he had been in trouble with the law several times, and he did not graduate. In the evenings Neal worked at the **Gates Rubber Company** at **999 South Broadway**, recapping tires, a trade that he would fall back on repeatedly in future years. Neal's brother, Jack, worked as a bartender at **Paul's Place**, a bar and restaurant at **2376 15th Street and Platte** that is now called **My Brother's Bar**. The bar proudly displays several Cassady and Kerouac items.

By the summer of 1945, Neal had dropped out of school and was on his own. One day when he was hanging out in the **Denver Public Library**, he met a boy named **Hal Chase**, home on vacation from Columbia University. They struck up a friendship and Neal promised to visit Chase in New York City, which he did during the winter of 1946–47. It was on that trip that Cassady met Jack Kerouac and Allen Ginsberg for the first time, before returning to Denver on March 4, 1947. For a while Neal rented a room at **1073 Downing Street** at $6 a week, and later he crashed with friends at **1830 Grant Street**. In his first letter back to Ginsberg from this address he asked Allen to send him stolen overcoats, which he promised he could sell in Denver. Also during March of 1947, **Bill Tomson**, a friend who lived at **1156 Gaylord**, introduced Neal Cassady to **Carolyn Robinson**. She was a graduate student at the **University of Denver** studying for her degree in fine arts and theater arts. While in Denver, Carolyn lived in the **Colburn Hotel** at **980 Grant Street** on the corner of Tenth. Following Tomson's introduction, Neal began to court Carolyn, successfully juggling a romance with her while continuing his relationship with LuAnne Henderson, his first wife.

b. When **Allen Ginsberg** arrived in June of 1947 hoping to pursue his own romantic affair with Cassady, he stayed in a nurses' dormitory with two more of Neal's girlfriends. Helen and Ruth Gullion lived on Grant Street, possibly at **1830 Grant**, the address Cassady used as his mail drop. In *On the Road* Kerouac transformed the Gullions into the Bettencourt sisters and depicted them both as waitresses. Since Ginsberg was penniless when he arrived, he began working as a night janitor for the **Daniels and Fisher Department Store** (later Mays) at **16th and Arapahoe Streets**. With the wages from that job Allen was able to rent a small basement room of his own on **Grant Street** in an old red brick rooming house. Kerouac described Ginsberg's Spartan cell as being "like the room of a Russian saint." In that room Ginsberg wrote the poems he came to call *The Denver Doldrums*. One morning Neal came into Allen's room and told him that everything had finally been straightened out. He was going to divorce LuAnne, marry Carolyn, and go with Allen to visit Burroughs in Texas.

c. During that same summer of 1947, **Jack Kerouac** also made his first trip to Denver to visit Hal Chase and Neal Cassady. In *On the Road* he described that long hitchhiking trip from New York City. After his final ride dropped him in Denver on **Larimer Street**, "I stumbled along with the most wicked grin of joy in the world among the old bums and beat cowboys." The first thing Kerouac did was to call Hal Chase, who had arranged for him to stay with **Allan Temko**. Temko was living in **Ed White**'s apartment at **1475 Cherry Street**. A few years later in 1951, it was Ed White who suggested to Kerouac that he sketch in words, just as an artist sketches with a pencil. This idea was pivotal in the development of Kerouac's spontaneous writing style.

On that trip Kerouac hung out in **Charlie Brown's Bar and Grill** at **980 Grant Street**, which is still in business. He also spent time thinking about Neal Cassady's childhood, which led him to a baseball field at the corner of **23rd and Welton Streets**. There, "a softball game was going on under the floodlights which also illuminated the gas tank," he wrote in *On the Road*.

Two years after his first visit to Denver, Kerouac decided to move his mother, sister, and brother-in-law there. He had just received an advance for his first book, *The Town and the City*, and as a result he had enough money to rent a nice little house in the suburb of Lakewood at **6100 West Center Place**. Until Jack's mother arrived in June of 1949, he lived in the **Denver YMCA** at **25 East 16th Street**. Once Gabrielle arrived, she decided that she didn't like the house Jack had found and stayed less than a month before taking the train home. While Kerouac was living at the Lakewood house alone, his editor Robert Giroux came to visit, and Jack took him "on the road" to experience hitchhiking first-hand. In 1947 Jack had toyed with the idea of working in the **Denargo Produce Market** on **Denargo Street**, but it wasn't until this 1949 trip that he actually got a job here. The back-breaking work he describes in *On the Road* was so exhausting that he lasted only a few days.

After the publication of *The Town and the City*, Harcourt Brace agreed to pay Kerouac's expenses to come to Denver from New York for a book signing. In May 1950, he appeared at the **Denver Dry Goods Company** at **16th and California Streets**, where all of his local friends turned out to support him. After the signing Jack went with Ed White and Bob and Beverly Burford to smoke some grass in the **Elitch Gardens** amusement park and then on to a party in his honor. Justin Brierly and Neal Cassady showed up, and the party continued until Kerouac left for Mexico City.

d. There are a few other local events of importance. In August 1976 **Billy Burroughs Jr.** received a liver transplant in the **Denver General Hospital**. Poet and editor **Robin Blaser** was born here on May 18, 1925, although he spent most of his childhood in Idaho. Another poet, **Ed Dorn**, died in Denver of pancreatic cancer on December 10, 1999.

2. Berthoud Pass. Crossing the Continental Divide on **Route 40** west of Denver is the high-altitude (11,307 ft.) Berthoud Pass. On one trip back to Denver from San Francisco, Neal Cassady took the wheel of a car at Craig, Colorado, and drove as fast as he could over this pass toward Denver. As Kerouac described it in *On the Road,* it was "a tremendous Gibraltarian door shrouded in clouds." Neal took the pass at top speed and then turned off the engine to save gas and sped down the mountain, passing every vehicle on the road.

3. Boulder.

a. In 1974, **Chögyam Trungpa**, a Tibetan lama, founded the first Buddhist college in America, naming it the **Naropa Institute** in honor of the eleventh-century abbot of the Nalanda University in India. Trungpa asked Allen Ginsberg and Anne Waldman to head his poetics program, and together they organized the **Jack Kerouac School of Disembodied Poetics**. For the next twenty-three years, until his death in 1997, Naropa occupied more of Ginsberg's time and energy than anything else. During those years he invited everyone associated

Left to right: Peter Orlovsky, Lawrence Ferlinghetti, William S. Burroughs, Gregory Corso, John Clellon Holmes, Allen Ginsberg, Carl Solomon, and Robert Frank (seated) on the porch of the Columbine Lodge, 1982

with the Beat Generation to visit Naropa to teach courses, and they all came. One of the largest events was the twenty-fifth anniversary celebration of *On the Road*, which Naropa hosted in July 1982. During the conference many of the Beats stayed at the **Columbine Lodge** on **Primrose Road** in the Chautauqua camp up the hill. They all spent time sitting on the wide front porch, reminiscing and swapping stories. In 1993 the college library at **2130 Arapahoe Avenue** was dedicated as the **Allen Ginsberg Library**.

Over the years Naropa has used several buildings in town for classes. Ginsberg's first poetry classes were held in **Casey Junior High School** at **13th and High Streets,** while many of the college offices were on the downtown mall at **1111 Pearl Street**. Later Naropa was able to purchase its own campus in the former public school buildings at **2130 Arapahoe Avenue**.

Allen Ginsberg and **Peter Orlovsky** lived in many places in Boulder, including the **Varsity Townhouse**

*"Bathing Beauties" Allen Ginsberg, Philip Whalen, and William S.
Burroughs at the pool in Boulder*

Photograph by Gordon Ball

Apartments at **1555 Broadway** as well as apartments
on **Pine Street, 1439 Mapleton Avenue**, and **2141 Bluff
Street**. In the mid-1980s Ginsberg sometimes stayed at
the home of friend David Padwa at **1001 Mapleton**.

The co-founder of the Jack Kerouac School, **Anne
Waldman**, lived in Boulder even longer than Allen
Ginsberg. It was due to Waldman's steadfast, hard work
that the school was able to accomplish so much. She
was the foundation upon which the poetics department
rested. Some other long-term residents of Boulder who
frequently taught at Naropa were William Burroughs,
Gregory Corso, Harry Smith, Anselm Hollo, Peter
Lamborn Wilson, and Steven Taylor, Allen's musical
accompanist.

b. **William Burroughs Jr. (Billy)** was a writer like his
father. His books *Speed* and *Kentucky Ham* tell about
his generation of drug users in America. Billy came to
Naropa in August 1976 to give a reading, and while in
Colorado he suffered severe liver failure. He received
one of the first liver transplants in the country from

surgeons in Denver. As a result of his medical situation, Billy remained in the area for the next four years. He tried to kick his addictions to alcohol and drugs, but was unsuccessful. His father, William Burroughs, came to teach at Naropa in 1976–78 to be closer to his sick son, but he was not a good role model for anyone trying to kick a habit. In 1981 Billy died as a direct result of his unabated alcoholism.

4. Buena Vista. In July 1944, eighteen-year-old **Neal Cassady** was sentenced to a year in the **Colorado State Reformatory** at Buena Vista for receiving stolen goods (a set of tires). While in jail, he went to the prison library and began to read the classics. By the time he was paroled in June of 1945, he had completed whatever education he would ever have.

5. Central City. Since 1932, an opera festival has been held in Central City every summer. **Jack Kerouac** went to the opera company's production of *Fidelio* with his friends Bob Burford and Ed White during his first visit to Denver in 1947. They all pitched in to clean out an abandoned miner's shack on the edge of town, where they threw big parties that weekend. Those parties formed an important part of the adventure Jack recalled in *On the Road*. **Justin Brierly**, the Columbia alumnus who had helped Hal Chase get into college, was a staunch supporter of the opera until his death in 1985. Brierly was also Neal Cassady's benefactor and helped him out of several scrapes.

6. Deer Trail. In the late spring of 1949, **Jack Kerouac** decided that he and his mother would move to Colorado, so in May he headed for Denver to begin looking for a place to live. Before reaching Denver, the bus stopped for a few minutes in the tiny town of Deer Trail, and Jack realized it was exactly the type of place he had in mind.

He wrote to Hal Chase that somewhere near Deertrail [sic] he had seen "the sun blushing through storm clouds upon a territorial area of brown plains where only one single farmhouse stood." That farmhouse was symbolic of the type of isolated retreat Kerouac dreamed of owning someday.

Denver (see Colorado location 1).

7. Farasita. At the end of August 1977, **Allen Ginsberg** and **Peter Orlovsky** took a break from the commotion caused by the Naropa poetry wars (see the entry for Snowmass, Colorado). They visited the **Libre Commune** in Farasita near Pueblo for a ten-day retreat. There they both marveled at the beautiful and peaceful mountains overlooking the Huerfano Valley. The success of this commune was a sharp contrast to the failed Cherry Valley farm that Ginsberg had tried to organize in upstate New York.

8. Fort Logan. **Neal Cassady** was placed in the **J.K. Mullen Home for Boys** at **3601 South Lowell Boulevard** in the summer of 1940. It was hoped that after his mother died, Neal would benefit from the peaceful surroundings and they would curb his juvenile delinquent tendencies. However, at the end of December 1940, Neal stole some athletic equipment and ran away from the institution.

9. La Junta. **Ken Kesey** was born in the high plains town of La Junta on September 17, 1935, to parents Fred and Geneva Smith Kesey. They raised him in a strict Christian home and taught him basic moral values through the examples found in the Bible and in folk tales. In 1946, when he was eleven, the family moved to a farm in Oregon. Except for a few years in the Palo Alto area near Stanford University, Kesey lived in Oregon for most of his life and died there in 2001.

10. Longmont. On **Jack Kerouac**'s first trip to Denver he paused in Longmont just long enough to take a nap on the lawn beside a service station under "a tremendous old tree." He noted how beautiful the small town was and how very attractive the Colorado girl was who made him an ice cream milkshake at the local diner. As usual he was in a hurry, so he stuck out his thumb, caught a ride, and moved on.

11. Padroni. In early 1946, before he met Kerouac and Ginsberg, **Neal Cassady** found a job on **Ed Uhl**'s ranch in Padroni, near Sterling. As a ranch hand he lasted only a few months, but the experience gave him a taste of the cowboy life and plenty of stories to tell. In *On the Road,* Kerouac incorporates some of Neal's tales about Ed Uhl, whom he refers to as Ed Wall.

12. Peetz. Neal Cassady's first wife, **LuAnne Henderson**, said that she was born in the kitchen of her grandmother's house in Peetz. Soon after she married Neal in July 1946, the couple spent a week in Peetz honeymooning, deciding what they would do next with their lives.

13. Red Feather Lakes. The **Rocky Mountain Dharma Center** (now called the Shambhala Mountain Center) in Red Feather Lakes was the site of several Buddhist retreats attended by **Allen Ginsberg, Peter Orlovsky, Anne Waldman**, and others from the Naropa Institute community. The center was founded in 1970 by Chögyam Trungpa as part of his Shambhala organization. Many of Ginsberg's poems were written while he was on retreat here, including one titled "221 Syllables at Rocky Mountain Dharma Center." A Tibetan shrine (*stupa*) was erected on the property, and it contains one-third of the ashes from the cremation of Allen Ginsberg, the ashes of Peter Orlovsky, and the ashes of Billy Burroughs Jr.

Peter Orlovsky, Allen Ginsberg, and friends blocking the tracks at Rocky Flats

14. Rocky Flats. During the late 1970s and 1980s, numerous demonstrations were held in an attempt to close the Rockwell nuclear weapons factory here. As many as 17,000 people took part in single marches, including **Allen Ginsberg, Peter Orlovsky,** and **Anne Waldman**, who sat on the railroad tracks to block weapons shipments. Protesting the manufacture of plutonium triggers for nuclear weapons, Anne Waldman wrote a song, "Uh-Oh Plutonium," and Ginsberg wrote the long poem "Plutonian Ode." Another poet, **Gregory Corso**, also read for the Rocky Flats Coalition in 1981, and **Daniel Ellsberg** led a group of marchers in 1978. In 1988 the government finally closed the plant and began to clean up the toxic waste.

15. Snowmass. In the fall of 1975 a notorious incident occurred during a three-month Buddhist retreat at **Snowmass Village** near Aspen. Poets **W.S. Merwin** and **Dana Naone** were guests of **Chögyam Trungpa** at the

Vajradhatu Seminary retreat that year. They had been given special dispensation to attend, even though they did not have the required background training for the seminary. When they refused to attend a Halloween party thrown by Trungpa, he ordered his Vajra guards to forcibly strip the couple and bring them naked to the party. This created a scandal in the Buddhist community, and many poets throughout the country took sides in the controversy, which became known as the Naropa Poetry Wars. Ed Sanders and Tom Clark both wrote books critical of Trungpa, and the backlash continued to affect Naropa's enrollment and fundraising efforts for years.

16. Woody Creek. Reporter and "gonzo" journalist **Hunter S. Thompson** made Woody Creek his home from 1968 until his death on February 20, 2005. On that date he committed suicide at **Owl Farm**, the house in Woody Creek that he described as his own "fortified compound." Thompson acknowledged that his method of writing owed a good deal to the spontaneity exemplified by Beat authors. He also became one of the first reporters to include himself as an essential part of his own news stories; he called this "gonzo journalism." During work on his first book, *Hell's Angels*, he came in contact with Michael McClure, Ken Kesey, and the Merry Pranksters and introduced them to the Angels. He was also a close friend of William S. Burroughs, with whom he shared a love of firearms, alcohol, and drugs.

MONTANA

1. Big Timber. Jack Kerouac passed through Big Timber on a February 1949 trip. There he saw a young, one-armed cowboy sitting amidst a group of old men at an inn. He carefully recorded this and everything else he saw in his pocket notebook, later incorporating his observations into *On the Road.*

2. Billings. On the same bus trip through Montana, **Jack Kerouac** described a stop at a cafeteria in Billings where he saw three girls eating with "their grave boyfriends." In his journal he noted that people could have their Utopian orgies if they wanted them, but save the ones with the Montana girls for him.

3. Butte.

a. On an overnight stop in subfreezing Butte during his long 1949 bus ride, **Jack Kerouac** fell in with some drunken Indians. He spent the night in a wild bar that he felt would be an ideal hangout for someone like Bill Burroughs. A card dealer with a big red nose in the saloon reminded him of a cross between his own father and W.C. Fields.

b. In 1972, **Allen Ginsberg** passed through Butte. On this particular trip he met a copper mine employee who reminded him of a young Neal Cassady. At three o'clock in the morning, the man "borrowed" a dump truck from the Anaconda Mining Company and recklessly drove Allen down into the giant **Berkeley copper pit**, much to Ginsberg's terror and delight.

4. Miles City. On February 7, 1949, **Jack Kerouac**'s bus from Portland, Oregon, pulled into Miles City, where Jack explored the empty streets just after a blizzard. In a drugstore window he saw the book *Yellowstone Red* by Tom Ray for sale and realized that regional tales like that were exactly the kind of stories he wanted to write.

IDAHO

1. Boise. **Rick and Rosemary Ardinger** are the owners and editors of Limberlost Press at **17 Canyon Trail** in Boise. Ever since the press began in 1976, Limberlost has published dozens of beautiful, finely printed books and broadsides by many writers. Robert Creeley, Ed Dorn, Lawrence Ferlinghetti, Allen Ginsberg, John Clellon Holmes, Jack Kerouac, and Gary Snyder are all well represented by Limberlost publications.

2. Caldwell. Caldwell is the home of the **College of Idaho**. Poet **Robin Blaser** attended the college for a year, but did not graduate.

3. Hailey. The literary lion **Ezra Weston Loomis Pound** was born in Hailey on October 30, 1885. The Ezra Pound birthplace is now the **Hailey Cultural Center**, located at **Second Avenue and Pine Street**. Pound's family left Hailey when he was only fifteen months old and never returned, but the town is justly proud of its most famous son. Nearly every poet of the twentieth century was influenced by Pound in one way or another. Allen Ginsberg in particular was intent on keeping Pound's memory alive, and after visiting the decaying house in 1993, Ginsberg promoted the idea that it be protected. The Ezra Pound Association was founded two years later and has worked toward its preservation.

4. Idaho Falls. **Chandler Brossard** was born in Idaho Falls in 1922. He is most often associated with Greenwich Village, where he wrote his most famous books, including *Who Walk in Darkness*, an underground classic first published in 1952. The story portrays subterranean communities like those in the Village and North Beach inhabited by hipsters and Beats. Brossard himself shied away from any association with the Beats, but he was appreciated by many of them.

5. Pocatello. One of the many colleges where poet **Ed Dorn** taught was **Idaho State University** in Pocatello. Dorn was here from 1961 to 1965. He had studied at Black Mountain College and was much influenced by the work of Charles Olson.

6. St. Maries. Artist **Robert LaVigne** was born in St. Maries in 1928. The house in which he was born once stood in a green meadow near a stream, but that area has now become suburbanized. LaVigne is best known for his delicate portraits of Beat poets in San Francisco, created during the mid-1950s. In 1954 he met Allen Ginsberg and introduced him to his model Peter Orlovsky, who was to become Ginsberg's companion for the next forty years. A selection of LaVigne's work was shown to a large public for the first time in 1995 at the Whitney Museum's "Beat Culture and the New America 1950–1965" exhibition.

7. Twin Falls. **Robin Blaser** was born in Denver in 1925, but grew up north of Twin Falls in **Dietrich Village**. His childhood here was not an especially happy one. His strict father, a burly section foreman on the railroad, thought a life in the arts was a waste of time, but encouraged by his grandmother, Robin took piano lessons as a boy. Blaser recalled that his father intentionally sent him out the day before a recital to pick sugar beets. It left his hands too stiff and sore to play. In spite of his father's attempts to discourage him, Blaser attended the College of Idaho, where he studied poetry. In 1944 he left Idaho permanently for the San Francisco Bay Area where he met Robert Duncan and Jack Spicer. They all became leaders of the San Francisco Renaissance literary movement. In 1966, Blaser relocated permanently to Canada.

WYOMING

1. Cheyenne. On July 24, 1947, **Jack Kerouac** just happened to pass through town during Cheyenne's annual **Wild West Week** on his first *On the Road* trip. "Great crowds of businessmen, fat businessmen in boots and tengallon hats, with their hefty wives in cowgirl attire bustled and whooped on the wooden sidewalks of old Cheyenne," he wrote. Kerouac was looking for the true West, so he was disappointed by the commercial nature of the event.

2. Jackson Hole. Chögyam Trungpa chose the off season at the **Crystal Springs Inn** in **Teton Village** for one of his first Buddhist retreats in 1972. Allen Ginsberg attended the seminary and returned to the inn the following year for another retreat. During this period Ginsberg and Trungpa worked on plans to create a poetics department at the newly founded Naropa Institute in Boulder. James Laughlin, the publisher of New Directions Books, also kept a vacation home in Jackson Hole.

Chögyam Trungpa Rinpoche

3. Lusk. Not many people know that Allen Ginsberg had several girlfriends over the course of his life and, even in his last years, debated whether or not to have children. One of his girlfriends during the early fifties was an attractive, dark-haired painter named **Dusty Moreland**. She grew up in Lusk, Wyoming. Although she lived with Allen for a while, she was also romantically involved with Gregory Corso, Jack Kerouac, and other poets in New York's Greenwich Village.

NEVADA

1. Route I-80. After one all-night binge in San Francisco, **Jack Kerouac** and **Neal Cassady** hitched a ride back East. In *On the Road*, Jack depicted the driver of the car as a "tall thin fag" from Kansas and Neal noted that the Plymouth he drove was "effeminate." With the young man driving, the three crawled slowly across California to Sacramento, stopping many times along the way. Finally when they got to Sacramento, Neal took the wheel of the car and stepped on the gas. The miles began to fly past as he sped along and they shot through Reno, Battle Mountain, and Elko on their way to Denver, following the route of current Interstate 80.

2. Golconda. In September 1951, **Gary Snyder** enrolled in graduate school at Indiana University to study anthropology. To get to Bloomington from California, he hitchhiked 2,300 miles, part of the way along what is now I-80 through the desert from Winnemucca to Elko. As John Suiter suggests in his wonderful book *Poets on the Peaks,* Snyder began to read D.T. Suzuki's *Essays in Zen Buddhism: First Series* while waiting in the small mining town of Golconda. This book was to change Snyder's life and bring him a greater understanding of Zen Buddhism. "That was the end of my career as an anthropologist," Snyder would recall years later.

Courtesy of the City Lights Archive

Albert Saijo

3. Las Vegas.

a. In many ways, parts of Las Vegas were "beat" even before that term was coined. It still had a down-and-out side to it in 1959 when **Jack Kerouac, Lew Welch,** and **Albert Saijo** drove through on their way from San Francisco to New York. They rode in Welch's jeep, which he nicknamed "Willy" and wrote the name in the dust on the tailgate. The trio stopped in town only long enough for Lew to lose $22. On this trip the three poets made up spontaneous haikus and poems that were published later by Don Allen's Grey Fox Press as *Trip Trap*.

b. In 1971 **Lawrence Ferlinghetti** read at the **University of Las Vegas** with the Russian poet **Andrei Voznesensky**. The two were put up at **Caesar's Palace** at **3570 Las Vegas Boulevard South**. Ferlinghetti showed the Russian poet how to play the slot machines, and Andrei won a hatful of silver dollars. Lawrence said that later Voznesensky told his friends back home how decadent he found the capitalists in America, but while he was here he had fully enjoyed the tacky opulence of his first-class room. Ferlinghetti was inspired by this trip to write his poem "Las Vegas Tilt."

4. Reno.

a. In the summer of 1955, shortly after **Peter Orlovsky** met Allen Ginsberg, Peter returned to New York to rescue his younger brother, Lafcadio, who was about to be committed to a mental hospital. Peter and Allen spent a weekend exploring the Yosemite area and then split up once they reached Reno. Orlovsky

Peter Orlovsky on Route 40 in Reno, preparing to hitch hike east, 1955

stood at the edge of town and began to hitchhike east on **Route 40**, and Ginsberg returned to San Francisco and wrote "Howl."

b. On August 14, 1978, **Philip Lamantia** and **Nancy Peters** were married by a Justice of the Peace in Reno's **Washoe County Courthouse** at **75 Court Street**. Afterwards, they went down to the Truckee River and drank champagne and danced. A few days later, the newlyweds drove to Virginia City, Nevada, the famous silver-mining boomtown.

UTAH

1. Salt Lake City. In *On the Road,* **Neal Cassady** revealed to Kerouac that he was born in Salt Lake City. "Dean [Kerouac's pseudonym for Neal in the book] is the perfect guy for the road because he actually was born on the road, when his parents were passing through Salt Lake City in 1926, in a jalopy, on their way to Los Angeles," Jack wrote. Although that is the romantic version of the story Cassady wanted to project, his real-life birth was more mundane. He was born to Maude Scheuer Cassady on February 8, 1926, in the **Salt Lake County General Hospital**, not in the back seat of a car. His father, Neal Sr., was working as a barber at the Desert Gym at the time, and they lived at **48½ Broadway**.

ARIZONA

1. Benson. In *On the Road,* **Neal Cassady, Jack Kerouac,** and **LuAnne Henderson** ran out of money on their trip back from New Orleans. They hoped that Jack would be able to borrow some money from his friend Alan Harrington in Tucson, so they mapped their course through Arizona. As they came into Benson, Jack was behind the wheel without a driver's license and nearly out of gas. At the top of a long hill, he put the car in neutral and coasted down the mountain into the first filling station he came to. There he pawned his watch for a dollar's worth of gas. Just as he was about to drive off, a state trooper appeared and asked to see Kerouac's identification. Frightened to see Neal and LuAnne in the backseat under a blanket, the trooper pulled his gun and ordered them to get out with their hands up. After the drama, he found that all their papers were in order except for Jack's lack of a license. By way of apology the officer said that Benson wasn't such a bad town. "You might enjoy it if you had breakfast here," he suggested. Without money they couldn't think of breakfast anywhere and headed straight for Tucson with Neal once again behind the wheel.

2. Bisbee.

a. Poet **Alice Notley** was born at the **Copper Queen Hospital** at **101 Cole Avenue** in Bisbee on November 8, 1945. Her father owned a store at **8 Brewery Gulch** at the time. When Alice was two, the family moved to Needles, California, just across the state line, where she grew up. In 1967 she left for New York's Barnard College and met the poet Ted Berrigan, whom she married in 1972.

Lawrence Ferlinghetti, left, at the Bisbee Poetry Festival

b. For seven years, from 1979 to 1985, Bisbee hosted an annual poetry festival. The first year poet **Lawrence Ferlinghetti** was the featured speaker, and on that occasion the festival organizers printed his chapbook *Mule Mountain Dreams,* which contained poems inspired by Bisbee. He was followed in 1980 by **Allen Ginsberg**, who irritated the town fathers by using four-letter words during his reading.

c. **John Mitchell**, once the manager of the celebrated Gaslight Cafe, the quintessential Greenwich Village coffeehouse of the late 1950s, died in Bisbee in 1997. His cafe had hosted readings by all the Beat poets from Allen Ginsberg and Gregory Corso to LeRoi Jones and Diane Di Prima. As the coffeehouse scene faded, the Gaslight closed and Mitchell moved on to retirement in Bisbee.

Philip Lamantia with Hopi Katchina dolls, 1972

Photograph by Nancy Peters

3. Oraibi. In 1971, after leaving Gary Snyder's house in the Sierra foothills the day after the official search for the missing Lew Welch was abandoned, **Philip Lamantia, Nancy Peters,** and **Don Allen** journeyed through the Southwest. The high point of the trip was a visit to Hopi pueblos, where they witnessed spring kachina ceremonies. On later trips to Hopi pueblos, Lamantia and Peters visited the author of *Sun Chief,* Don C. Talayesva, and spent time with Hopi poet Ramson Lomatewama and artist friends. Lamantia's impressions of Hopi life and ritual figured prominently in many poems, such as "Orabi." In 1981, Nancy and Philip helped organize a benefit to support the traditional Navajo and Hopi peoples whose land was being ruthlessly exploited by Peabody Coal.

4. Phoenix. Beat poet **Lew Welch** was born in Phoenix on August 16, 1926. Not long after his birth his parents, Lewis Barrett and Dorothy Brownfield Welch, separated. Lew and his sister were then brought up by his mother in California. In 1959 Welch and **Albert Saijo** drove **Jack Kerouac** from San Francisco to New York and passed through Phoenix on the way. They wrote a collaborative poem that was published in 1973 as *Trip Trap: Haiku on the Road.* On that same trip, the trio stopped at a white roadside cross that marked the site of a fatal accident. Welch pulled the memorial from the ground and took it along with them to New York, where it was ceremoniously hung on Allen Ginsberg's wall.

Lew Welch and Allen Ginsberg

191

5. Quartzsite. On one of the later cross-country drives that **Jack Kerouac** described in *On the Road,* he recognized the names of the towns he passed from an earlier 1947 bus trip across the desert on Route 60. As he headed back to California this time he saw towns like Wickenburg, Salome, and Quartzsite, from the window of the speeding car instead of a slow Greyhound bus.

6. Tempe. Tempe is the home of **Arizona State University**. The Special Collections Department in the university library contains an extensive archive of William S. Burroughs material, including manuscripts and correspondence. It also holds other important Beat-related collections, such as the papers of poet and translator Claude Pelieu and the research material used by Ted Morgan for his book *Literary Outlaw: The Life and Times of William S. Burroughs.*

7. Tucson.

a. **Joanna Kinnison** (later McClure) was born on November 10, 1930, in a house called "The Stork's Nest" on **Speedway** in Tucson. When she was a few months old her family returned to their eighty-section ranch named the **U Circle Ranch**. It stretched from the Catalina Mountains above Oracle into the valley below, where raising cattle in dry country required a lot of open land. Joanna attended **University Heights Elementary School** and went to **Mansfield Junior High** and **Tucson Senior High School**. While she was studying at the **University of Arizona** she met Michael McClure, whom she married in 1954. Typical of many of the creative women of her era, Joanna wrote secretly in her journal, too modest to show her work to the male writers around her, and they were too insensitive to inquire. Later, books like *Wolf Eyes*, published in 1974, would reveal her own interest in spirituality and her love of nature.

b. Although born in Newton, MA, in 1919, **Alan Harrington** spent most of his adult life in Tucson. Jack Kerouac referred to him as the novelist Hal Hingham in *On the Road*. In the late 1940s Neal Cassady and Kerouac stopped at Harrington's home on **Fort Lowell Road** to borrow some money for their trip back to California. "We passed innumerable Mexican shacks in the shady sand till a few adobe houses appeared," wrote Kerouac about the drive out to his house. Their visit, described in much greater detail in the original scroll version of *On the Road*, made Harrington a local celebrity. In 1966 Alan wrote his own novel, *The Secret Swinger*, in which he used his New York friend Bill Cannastra as the model for the character Bill Genovese. In 1997 Harrington died of leukemia in Tucson and his ashes were scattered on a hillside just outside Oracle, a few miles to the north.

c. In 1953 **Michael McClure** transferred from the University of Wichita to the **University of Arizona** at **1401 East University Boulevard**. Here he took upper-level Physical Anthropology classes, and learned more through those studies than from anything else in his academic career. McClure also was given permission from J.P. Scott to attend his graduate-level classes in art where he began to paint abstract expressionist canvases, a style unknown in Tucson at the time. While at the university, Michael met his future wife Joanna just about the time she moved to San Francisco, and he decided to follow her there.

In 1969 **Allen Ginsberg** was involved in a particularly unpleasant incident while visiting the **University of Arizona**. Here he held a press conference at the **Ruth Stephan Poetry Center, 1508 E. Helen Street**. One of the reporters got into a heated debate with Ginsberg over the subject of homosexuality, and during the argument that followed Allen called the reporter a "cocksucker." In his rage, the reporter punched Ginsberg in the mouth, an act that made national news.

NEW MEXICO

1. Albuquerque.

a. After **Robert Creeley** left Black Mountain College in 1956, he found a job teaching junior high students at the **Albuquerque Academy for Boys**, then located in the basement of a small church. He rented an inexpensive three-room adobe house at **601 Montano N.W.** Even though he was engaged as a teacher, Creeley was paid only a janitor's wages because his B.A. was no from an accredited college. Charles Olson tried to help him by sending him an "official" degree from Black Mountain College, but Creeley's employer would not accept it. In the end he had to go back to the University of New Mexico for his accredited master's degree, which he received in 1960.

b. In 1957, when **Bobbie Louise Hawkins** decided to

Robert Creeley

marry Robert Creeley, she lived at **1826 Griegos**. At first the couple lived together in Alameda, just north of Albuquerque, but in September 1960, they found a two-story house at **1835 Dartmouth N.E.** closer to Creeley's school. A few weeks after they moved into this house, their young daughter Leslie was killed in a tragic accident in the backyard when a dirt bank collapsed on top of her. In 1961, Creeley began teaching at the **University of New Mexico** on **Las Lomas Road N.E.** where he remained for several years.

c. **Gregory Corso** also taught a term at the **University of New Mexico** in the spring of 1970. Corso had married Belle Carpenter, who was living near Santa Fe in **Tesuque** at the time, so he moved in with her. Things never went smoothly for Corso, and before long he ended up in a Santa Fe jail and separated from his wife.

d. **Allen Ginsberg** passed through New Mexico frequently and in 1970 he stayed with poet Nanao Sakaki for a longer visit. Allen had first met Nanao in Japan in 1963 through their mutual friend Gary Snyder, and the two poets quickly became friends.

e. **Jan Kerouac**, Jack Kerouac's daughter, died at the age of 44 in an Albuquerque hospital in June 1996 after a long struggle with kidney disease. The sadness of Jan's short life was that her father never acknowledged his paternity; in fact, they only met in person twice. Jan also became a writer. Her best-known work is *Baby Driver*, which tells of her own life "on the road."

2. Las Cruces. In *On the Road*, **Jack Kerouac** mentioned Las Cruces a few times as he passed through it on all his cross-country trips via the southern route. When **Neal Cassady** drove the Hinkles to the East Coast on an early trip, he impulsively decided to detour north through Denver while "roaring through Las Cruces." Although he had recently married his second wife, Carolyn, he picked up his first wife, LuAnne Henderson, to travel with them just for kicks. On the way back, Kerouac and Cassady passed through Las Cruces in the middle of the night, "the same Las Cruces that had been Neal's pivot on the way east," Jack noted.

3. Los Alamos. In September 1929 **William S. Burroughs** was sent to the **Ranch School**, a boarding school founded by Mr. Ashley Pond near Los Alamos. At the time it was a 900-acre ranch in the middle of nowhere. Burroughs, who suffered from sinus problems, went to school in New Mexico for his health and stayed here until 1931. "I was forced to become a Boy Scout, eat everything on my plate, exercise before breakfast, sleep on a porch in zero weather, stay outside all afternoon, ride a sullen, spiteful, recalcitrant horse twice a week and all day on Saturday," Burroughs was to complain later. His mother came to visit him in April 1931, two months before his graduation, and he persuaded her to take him home. As a result, he didn't graduate from the Ranch School, but finished his high school education back in St. Louis. In 1943 the Ranch School was taken over by the Manhattan Project and became part of the larger Los Alamos National Laboratory, where the atom bombs that destroyed Hiroshima and Nagasaki were developed.

4. Placitas. In May 1963, **Robert Creeley** moved into a house with a swimming pool in this town about twenty miles north of Albuquerque. Allen Ginsberg and Peter Orlovsky visited him here as they drove cross-country from California to New York in their Volkswagen bus. On that trip they camped out along the road and stayed with friends whenever they could. February 1, 1966, the day they arrived in Placitas, was the day that LSD was officially outlawed in the United States and that dominated their conversation.

5. Raton. Near the end of the story in *On the Road,* Neal Cassady and Jack Kerouac made a mad dash for the Mexican border and went through Raton on their way. Kerouac noted that they "passed the rounded rocks of Raton and stopped at a diner ravingly hungry for hamburgers, one of which we wrapped in a napkin not to eat till over the border below."

6. Santa Fe.

a. In 1972, Viking Press asked **Allen Ginsberg** to write an introduction for Jack Kerouac's book *Visions of Cody,* which was to be published posthumously. Allen had just been in Montana, and drove down to Santa Fe with his friend, a Buddhist nun named Tsultrim Allione. On the trip he reread not only *Visions,* but *On the Road,* too, just to refresh his memory.

Ginsberg returned to Santa Fe a few years later on a weeklong trip with his father, Louis, and stepmother, Edith, planning to visit friends Ram Dass and David Padwa, a fellow Buddhist. On that trip he also ran into Chögyam Trungpa, who was to become his guru for the next fifteen years. During those years Ginsberg

Ram Dass, Allen Ginsberg, and Chögyam Trungpa in Santa Fe

co-directed the poetics department at Trungpa's Naropa Institute in Boulder with Anne Waldman.

b. In 1984, Roshi Richard Baker, the head of San Francisco's Zen Center, asked **Philip Whalen** to work at his center in Santa Fe. Whalen, a Buddhist teacher as well as a poet, was only too happy to oblige and stayed there for the next three years.

7. Taos. Robert Creeley spent some time in Taos during the summer of 1956 with Marthe Rexroth. She had left her husband, Kenneth Rexroth, in San Francisco after falling in love with Creeley. Their relationship was short-lived and Marthe returned to Kenneth within a few months. As a result Rexroth harbored a grudge against many of the Beat writers for years. Oddly enough, he forgave Creeley, but never forgave Kerouac for what he imagined was Jack's role in the drama. In August 1982, the First Annual Taos Poetry Circus was held, featuring readings by Allen Ginsberg, Gregory Corso, and Peter Orlovsky.

Gary Snyder

VIII. Pacific States

OREGON

1. Portland.

a. On October 20, 1923, **Philip Whalen** was born in Portland. October 20 was coincidentally his mother's birthday. Philip's father worked as a traveling salesman for the **Honeyman Hardware Company** at **555 N.W. Park Avenue** in Portland, so the family moved around quite a bit. When he was two, the Whalens moved to Centralia, Washington and then two years later moved

Photograph by D. Sorensen, courtesy of the City Lights Archive

Philip Whalen and Lloyd Reynolds

back to Oregon and settled in The Dalles. Determined to provide Philip with a stable home life, the family managed to stay there until Philip graduated from high school. After Whalen's mother passed away in 1941, he and his father returned to Portland, but like so many young men of his generation Philip enlisted in the U.S. Army Air Corps during World War II and shipped out.

b. Twelve-year-old **Gary Snyder** moved with his family to Portland around 1942. While he was a student at **Lincoln High School** at **1600 S.W. Salmon Street**, from which he graduated in 1947, Gary worked as a copyboy for the *Portland Oregonian*. During the summers he spent all his spare time in the forests and hiked to the summits of many peaks in the Oregon and Washington Cascades.

c. In 1946, when **Philip Whalen** returned from military service, he enrolled as a freshman at **Reed College** at **3203 S.E. Woodstock Boulevard**, supported by the G.I. Bill. He enjoyed his professors, especially Lloyd

Reynolds, who taught English literature and helped shape Whalen's literary tastes. Whalen graduated in 1951 with a B.A. in anthropology and literature. Whalen's senior thesis was titled "The Dimensions of a Haida Myth."

In 1947 **Gary Snyder** entered Reed College and graduated with the class of 1951 alongside Whalen. As a student at Reed, Snyder became close friends not only with Whalen but with fellow students **Lew Welch** and **Dell Hymes**. After he left Reed, Hymes went to Indiana University, and Snyder followed him there intending to study anthropology at the graduate level. In 1949, while they were all students at Reed, Snyder, Whalen, and Welch lived together in an apartment at **1414 S.E. Lambert Street**.

Lew Welch transferred to Reed in 1948 and soon met Snyder and Whalen. By the autumn of 1949 Welch was co-editing the college literary magazine, *Janus*. In 1950, after graduation, Lew moved into an apartment at **49 S.W. First Avenue** with the painter Ed Danielson.

Allen Ginsberg read at Reed with Snyder on an early trip to the Pacific Northwest in 1956. The college recorded Ginsberg's reading, but the tape of that event was lost until 2008. It is the earliest known recording of Ginsberg reading his landmark poem "Howl."

Allen and Gary returned to Reed once more in August 1965. After speaking to students they went to the **Portland Coliseum** to hear the Beatles in concert. Ginsberg described the pandemonium he found there in his poem "Portland Coliseum." John Lennon acknowledged Ginsberg in the audience, an honor Allen deeply appreciated.

In late May 1967, less than two years after the Beatles concert, Ginsberg was back in Portland once more, this time to give a reading at **Portland State**

Courtesy of the Allen Ginsberg Trust

Gary Snyder and Allen Ginsberg hiking in the Pacific Northwest, 1965

University. On that occasion the students ran an article about him in the school newspaper, illustrating it with the famous nude portrait of Ginsberg and Orlovsky by Richard Avedon. It created a minor scandal, and that issue of the newspaper was suppressed by the college administration. Once again Ginsberg was prompted to speak out against censorship and in defense of the sanctity of the nude human body.

2. Crater Lake. In 1965, **Allen Ginsberg, Gary Snyder**, and Gary's girlfriend Martene Algiers took a monthlong camping trip through the Pacific Northwest. Along the way they stopped to see Crater Lake. The dramatic natural beauty of the area made a profound impression on Ginsberg, who remarked that he had never seen anything as "Godlike" and noble before in his life.

3. The Dalles. In the town of The Dalles, two thieving hobos **Jack Kerouac** had met in Portland stepped off his bus and into a blizzard that was sweeping up the Columbia River gorge. Back then, Jack didn't know that his future friend **Philip Whalen** had grown up in The Dalles. Whalen lived there from 1927 to 1941. While he was still a high school student in The Dalles he discovered Buddhism and began to study Buddhist texts in the local public library. Following the death of Whalen's mother, he and his father left his hometown for good.

4. Eugene.

a. As an undergraduate, **Ken Kesey** attended the **University of Oregon** before he headed off to Stanford, where fame and notoriety awaited him. Here he majored in speech and communications, excelled in wrestling, and acted in all the school plays. While Kesey was working on his degree in Eugene he married his high school sweetheart, Faye Haxby. Because Ken was an excellent student, he earned a Woodrow Wilson Fellowship award to Stanford for postgraduate work. After several years in California, Kesey returned to his farm in Oregon and frequently taught at the university. On November 10, 2001, Kesey died of liver cancer in Eugene's **Sacred Heart Medical Center**. A standing-room-only memorial service was held for him shortly thereafter in the **McDonald Theater** at **1010 Willamette Street**.

b. Although the **University of Oregon** is now a staunch supporter of Ken Kesey and the freedom of speech and expression he advocated, things were not always so. In 1964, the school's administration suspended publication of the *Northwest Review* after the sixth issue. It included work by Philip Whalen, Antonin Artaud, and Fidel Castro. The college labeled it "a filthy, obscene organ of atheism and leftism." The editors, James Koller, Edward van Aesstyn, and William Wroth, decided to create their own magazine instead of fighting the administration. They called it *Coyote's Journal*, and the first issue continued in the same vein, with work by Olson, Snyder, Loewinsohn, and Wakoski.

5. Lafayette. In the summer of 1955, following a mystical revelation in Mexico, **Philip Lamantia** went to live north of town at the Trappist **Abbey of Our Lady of Guadalupe** on **N.E. Abbey Road**. At the time the abbey had just relocated to Oregon from Pecos, New Mexico, and Lamantia discovered that the contemplative life suited him. In October 1955, while he was living at the abbey, he took a short break to visit San Francisco and read at the historic Six Gallery event. He returned to the Abbey intermittently over the next two years.

6. Mount Hood. Perhaps the most accomplished outdoorsman of the Beat Generation, **Gary Snyder** climbed snowcapped Mount Hood first in 1946 at the age of sixteen. By the time he was twenty-two he had climbed it fourteen times in all sorts of weather. That alone was more than enough to qualify him to join the Mazamas Mountain Club in Portland, a group devoted to hiking and climbing in the Pacific Northwest.

7. Newport. **Philip Whalen** was living in this small town on the rugged Oregon coast in the fall of 1958 when Jack Kerouac sent him the first copy of his new book, *The Dharma Bums*. Whalen's character in that book, the genial Warren Coughlin, was a calm counterpoint to the ever active person of Japhy Ryder, the main character Jack based on Gary Snyder. As soon as he received the book, Whalen read it from cover to cover and wrote Snyder that he thought it was a beautiful book. However he wanted to warn Gary that it might stir up all sorts of controversy in the Bay Area. Before Snyder left for Japan that fall, he stopped in to visit Whalen in Newport.

8. Pleasant Hill. In November 1967, following his release from the San Mateo County Sheriff's Honor Camp in California where he had served time on marijuana charges, **Ken Kesey** and his family moved to a farm in Pleasant Hill. For the rest of his life Kesey took pleasure in the simple country life he had known as a boy helping his father raise livestock. Kesey continued to write, but nothing ever reached the popularity of his first two books, *One Flew Over the Cuckoo's Nest* and *Sometimes a Great*

Notion. While living here in 1984, Kesey's son, Jed, was tragically killed in a highway accident as he traveled with his school wrestling team. Ken Kesey himself died in Oregon in 2001.

Portland (see Oregon location 1).

Ken Kesey and Allen Ginsberg

9. Springfield. From 1946 until he left for college, **Ken Kesey** lived in Springfield. He attended **Springfield High School** at **875 Seventh Street** and graduated with the class of 1953. Kesey was a good student and a star athlete who won several wrestling championships and was nearly selected for the U.S. Olympic wrestling team.

10. Waldport. During World War II, many conscientious objectors were sent to a special camp in Waldport that was operated by the Civilian Public Service of the Mennonite Central Committee. There they performed noncombat duties for the army. **William Everson** worked as a printer in the camp, and in addition to his regular job, he managed to publish two periodicals using the army's press, *The Tide* and *The Illiterati*. While acting as the director of the fine arts project at Waldport, Everson established the Untide Press. Untide was the name he used for everything that he wanted to publish that was not appropriate for *The Tide*, the camp's weekly paper. During his three and a half years in this camp he published his own poetry as well as that of fellow CO's Kenneth Patchen, Glen Coffield, and Jacob Sloan. The building in which Everson worked still remains on the corner of **Broadway and Grant Streets**.

11. Warm Springs. During the summer of 1951, when **Gary Snyder** was twenty-one, he worked as a lumber scaler on the **Warm Springs Indian Reservation**. Snyder was planning to attend graduate school in Indiana that fall to study anthropology, so while he was here he made notes about the Native American berry feast that was held on the reservation. The following year he wrote one of his first great poems, called simply "A Berry Feast." By the time he returned to work setting choke for the Warm Springs Lumber Company in the summer of 1954, he had given up the idea of becoming an anthropologist, as his interests turned more and more toward poetry and Buddhism.

WASHINGTON

1. Crater, Sauk, and Sourdough Mountains. In 1952 **Gary Snyder** was offered a summer job as a fire spotter on **Crater Mountain**. It was the perfect job for a poet, because the work was easy and afforded leisure time to read, write, and study. The following summer Snyder returned to the rugged North Cascades and was assigned to **Sourdough Mountain**. That year he brought his friend **Philip Whalen** along to be the lookout on **Sauk Mountain**. The next year Whalen took the job as fire spotter on Sourdough and liked that mountain so much that he returned again in 1955. Both poets memorialized the Sourdough Lookout in their poems. Snyder wrote "Mid-August at Sourdough Mountain Lookout" and Whalen wrote "Sourdough Mountain Lookout." **Marblemount** was the small town at the base of the mountains where they provisioned themselves for the long summer in isolation. The actual wooden lookout stations on these mountaintops have all but disappeared, but the one on Sourdough remains and has been placed on the National Register of Historic Places.

Photograph by John Suiter

Kerouac's fire-spotter cabin on Desolation Peak

2. Desolation Peak. This mountain peak in the Ross Lake National Recreation Area of the North Cascades National Park is where **Jack Kerouac** spent the summer of 1956 working as a fire spotter. It can only be reached by a strenuous seven-mile hike along the Desolation Peak Trail. Jack wrote about his experiences here in great detail in *Desolation Angels*. Gary Snyder and Philip Whalen encouraged him to take the job with the Forestry Service so that he could make money while still having time for reading and writing. Kerouac had to go first to Marblemount for provisions and then cross Ross Lake by boat to the foot of the long trail up the mountain. From his lookout he could see **Mt. Hozomeen** in the distance, a terrifying image that recurs in his writing. As soon as his sixty days were over, Kerouac gave up the peaceful solitude and headed back to the excitement and frenetic pace of city life.

3. Lake City. Between the ages of two and twelve, **Gary Snyder** lived on a marginally viable farm in Lake City, not far from Seattle. His family ran a small dairy and Gary's responsibilities included raising his own flock of chickens.

While growing up in this rural environment, he began to explore the forests and mountains of the Northwest wilderness.

4. Mt. Baker National Forest. In 1965 **Allen Ginsberg** accompanied **Gary Snyder** and his girlfriend Martene Algiers on a camping trip to the Pacific Northwest. They hiked up to Glacier Peak in the North Cascades on their way to Canada. It was a thrilling experience for Ginsberg, who, until then, had not been much of an outdoorsman.

5. Mt. St. Helen's. The white-capped volcano named Mt. St. Helen's was the first major peak that **Gary Snyder** climbed. Although he was just a teenager in 1945, he was already an experienced hiker and mountain climber. During the summers he worked in a YMCA camp in the area doing carpentry and grooming trails. In fact, Snyder said that he "first started writing poetry at 16, trying to capture the feeling of mountain-climbing."

Gary Snyder and Philip Whalen

6. Port Townsend. On May 17, 1999, filmmaker and writer **James Broughton** died in his home in picturesque Port Townsend overlooking the Strait of Juan de Fuca. He had lived there for a decade with his partner, Joel Singer. Broughton was buried in Port Townsend with an epitaph that reads, "Adventure—not predicament."

7. Seattle.
a. Michael McClure lived in Seattle from 1937 to 1941. When he was still a young boy, his parents divorced

and he was sent to live with his maternal grandparents in a house at **116th and Greenwood**. The area was still partially forested then and had little footpaths that afforded McClure a view of the Pacific Ocean. The outdoor life inspired in him deep feelings about the natural world. Later Michael lived with his mother and stepfather in a house at **5032 35th Street S.W.** That home was adjacent to an eighty-acre nature training camp complete with woodland paths that he could explore when he wasn't swimming in the nearby Lincoln Pool. During the war there were Victory Gardens all over his neighborhood, and Michael joined the other boys in stealing fruit from the trees as they acted out scenes from Robin Hood.

b. **Robert LaVigne**, the talented artist who originally introduced Allen Ginsberg to Peter Orlovsky, spent a good deal of his life in the area. He still lives and paints in his studio near the **Pike Street Market**.

c. In early 1956, on their tour of the Northwest, **Allen Ginsberg** and **Gary Snyder** gave a reading at the **University of Washington**. In a letter Allen embellished the event by saying that "a dozen gray-haired ladies rushed out screaming." Nonetheless they had a successful visit. Allen had been in the city before and enjoyed showing Gary the wonderful secondhand clothing stores he had discovered on **Skid Road.** Gary showed him the **Wobblie Union Hall** in the same neighborhood. Ginsberg's poem "Afternoon Seattle" describes that visit. "Psalm III" and "Tears" were also written in Seattle, a town that seemed to inspire Ginsberg.

d. In 1968 when **Philip Lamantia** and **Nancy Peters** returned to the United States from two years in Spain, they moved to Seattle while Nancy finished her Library Science degree. The couple first lived on **Calhoun Street**, a couple of blocks from Lake Washington and the Arboretum, before moving to **46th Street** on Phinney Ridge near the Woodland Park Zoo. From these homes they enjoyed excursions to the mountains and the ocean. While in Seattle, Philip wrote many of the poems published in *The Blood of the Air.*

e. **Nancy Peters**, the co-owner of City Lights Books, was born in Seattle, although her family lived in the small daffodil-growing town of Puyallup, twenty-five miles to the south, at the time of her birth. Both her parents were musicians and educators. She grew up at **6210 36th Avenue N.E.**, in Seattle's Ravenna neighborhood and attended **Roosevelt High School**, where she became editor of the school newspaper. She received her B.A. in literature from the **University of Washington**, graduating Phi Beta Kappa, and a decade later earned her graduate degree in library science there.

f. **Jack Kerouac** spent some time in Seattle and described his visit in *Desolation Angels*. He stayed at the **Hotel Stevens**, then on **First Avenue** near Skid Road, observing that the most important thing about it was that it had no bedbugs. The hotel has been torn down and replaced by the Jackson Federal Building. At a dollar seventy-five a night it was a good place for him to readjust to city life after spending two months in solitude as a fire spotter on Desolation Peak. Jack enjoyed the city and described every detail as he walked down First Avenue past Thom McAnn's shoe store and Grant's drugstore on his way to the burlesque house.

8. Skagit River. To get to his fire lookout job in June 1956, **Jack Kerouac** hitchhiked up the Skagit Valley, along this great river swollen with spring run-off. He worried that once on the lookout, he would not be able to survive without alcohol and suffered many nightmares as a result. To pass the time he wrote haiku as he traveled along the river.

9. Spokane. Writer **John Montgomery** was born in Spokane on May 2, 1919, to John McVey and Melle Murray Montgomery. He became a hiking partner for Kerouac and Snyder and is mentioned as Henry Morley in *The Dharma Bums* and as Alex Fairbrother in *Desolation Angels.* Montgomery wrote several memoirs about Kerouac, *Kerouac at the Wild Boar* and *The Kerouac We Knew.*

10. Tacoma. Author **Richard Brautigan** was born in Tacoma on January 30, 1935. His parents were Bernard F. Brautigan, a laborer, and Lulu Mary Keho Brautigan, a waitress, both of whom outlived their son. Before he was born his parents divorced, and he was raised a Catholic by his mother and her abusive new husband. Much of his unhappy childhood was spent in Eugene, Oregon, where he wrote his first poems.

CALIFORNIA

1. Alameda. For details about the sites in this area, please refer to *The Beat Generation in San Francisco,* pages 197–198.

2. Albany. For details about the sites in this area, please refer to *The Beat Generation in San Francisco,* pages 189–190.

3. Arcadia. On a bus ride to Los Angeles, **Jack Kerouac** met and fell in love with a beautiful Mexican girl named Bea Franco. The couple decided to hitchhike to New York together. That night, they walked a few miles through Arcadia to get out of the city center until finally they were "pointed towards that enormity which is the American continent." They had no luck finding a ride and ended up spending what little money they had on a hotel room. This rather sad story is told in *On the Road*, where Kerouac identifies Bea as Terry.

4. Bakersfield. In *On the Road*, **Jack Kerouac** describes how he first saw Bea Franco on a bench in the Bakersfield bus station in 1947. For the next two weeks he stayed with her and tried his hand at migrant labor, but the affair was not to last. After spending some time in Los Angeles they wound up back in Bakersfield looking for work. "The thought of living in a tent and picking grapes in the cool California mornings hit me right," Kerouac romantically wrote about the back-breaking work.

5. Berkeley. For details about the sites in this area, please refer to *The Beat Generation in San Francisco*, pages 190–196. Berkeley is also the home of the **University of California**, which hosted the Berkeley Poetry Conference in July 1965. It was a seminal gathering of Beat, Black Mountain, and Bay Area writers attended by Creeley, Duncan, Ginsberg, Kyger, Olson, Snyder, Welch, and Wieners, to name only a few. For the first time many younger writers like Anne Waldman and Ted Berrigan had a chance to interact with the older Beat poets in an academic setting. After it was over, Robert Creeley pronounced, "There will never be another poetry conference in Berkeley; Berkeley is too bizarre."

Gary Snyder at the Berkeley Poetry Conference, 1965

Photograph by Tove Neville, courtesy of the City Lights Archive

6. Big Sur and Bixby Canyon. For details about the sites in this area, please refer to *The Beat Generation in San Francisco,* pages 209–212.

8. Bolinas. For details about the sites in this area, please refer to *The Beat Generation in San Francisco*, pages 216–217.

9. Bridgeport. Not far to the northeast of Yosemite is the area where **Jack Kerouac, Gary Snyder,** and **John Montgomery** went hiking during *The Dharma Bums* period of October 1955. Their jumping-off point into the mountains was the town of Bridgeport, which Kerouac describes as a sleepy town with two restaurants, two gas stations, and a school, all clustered along **Highway 395**. Montgomery was unprepared for the cold mountain air and tried to buy a new sleeping bag in town, but couldn't find one. He borrowed blankets from the big, white-frame inn along **Twin Lakes**.

Montgomery stayed down in camp at the base of **Matterhorn Peak**, while Kerouac made it most of the way up in sneakers. Only Snyder succeeded in reaching the summit, a climb described in *The Dharma Bums*. On other occasions Snyder took long backpacking trips to the **Minarets** and the headwaters of the **Kern**, also in the area.

10. Davis. The Davis campus of the **University of California** dominates this small town. Many members of the Beat Generation have given readings at the college over the years. It was during a reading at the college in 1969 that **William Everson** announced he was leaving the priesthood. At the time Everson was better known as Brother Antoninus, who had been a lay brother of the Dominican Order since 1951. His conversion had been the result of a profound religious experience he underwent on Christmas Eve, 1948. In some ways it was similar to the visionary experiences of other Beat writers like Philip Lamantia and Allen Ginsberg.

Gary Snyder taught at UC Davis until his retirement in 2002, at which time he became professor emeritus. It was due to his efforts, friendships, and influence that many Beat writers visited Davis. Today, Snyder's enormous archive is one of the great treasures stored in the university library's Special Collections Department.

11. Dublin. In 1967 **Lawrence Ferlinghetti** spent nineteen days in Alameda County at the **Santa Rita Jail, 5325 Broder Boulevard**. He was arrested (along with Joan Baez's mother and many UC Berkeley students) during an anti–Vietnam War protest at the Oakland Army Induction Center. As an act of conscience Lawrence refused to post bail. While incarcerated, Ferlinghetti worked in the prison laundry and wrote "Santa Rita Blues," which begins with the lines, "A man in jail is nothing / and his name is Nada. . . ." When he left jail he smuggled his notebook out among his clothing and published it as soon as he could. Two years earlier, in March 1965, **Neal Cassady** had been arrested for a driving offense and temporarily put in the same jail. Santa Rita was also the minimum-security prison where artist **George Herms** spent six months following a 1958 arrest for selling a small amount of marijuana.

12. El Centro. Just prior to Christmas 1955, **Jack Kerouac** stopped at this border town hoping to catch the express freight train nicknamed the Zipper. After the conductor warned him about delays, Kerouac decided to hitchhike instead. Jack wound up spending a wild night of drinking and whoring across the border in Mexicali with the first driver who picked him up, but by Christmas Eve, Kerouac was safely back in his sister's house in Rocky Mount, North Carolina.

13. Fort Bragg. Philip Lamantia loved to visit the regions north of San Francisco around Fort Bragg and Clear Lake. Between 1976 and 1983 Lamantia spent a good deal of time in this area, and his poems from the period, such as "Native Medicine" and others collected in *Meadowlark West*, reference images from the rich Miwok and Pomo traditions and literature of this region.

14. Fresno.

a. Fresno is a crossroads for activity in the fertile San Joaquin Valley, and **Jack Kerouac** passed through the town many times on his trips. While he was living with a migrant worker named Bea Franco, Jack and Bea's friend Ponzo drove around this area in a smelly old truck looking for manure to pick up and resell. "Today we drink, tomorrow we work," Ponzo told Kerouac. It was exactly the kind of advice that Jack was happy to follow.

b. **Fresno State College** (now California State University at **5241 North Maple Avenue**) was the school **William Everson** attended in the early 1930s before his religious conversion. He dropped out, returned once, but did not graduate. It was here that he discovered the work of the poet Robinson Jeffers. Jeffers was to become a great influence on Everson's own writing and motivated him to become a poet himself.

15. Indio. To support his family, **Neal Cassady** worked for the Southern Pacific railroad as a brakeman and conductor. On several occasions, due to the nature of railroad work, he had to room far from the Bay Area, where Carolyn and their three children lived. Indio, in the Coachella Valley just east of Palm Springs, was one of those places. In 1953 he rented room #6 in **Webb's Rooming House** at **44-871 Towne Avenue**. For a while he worked on the Indio-Yuma line and spent what little free time he had writing letters to Carolyn back in San Jose. A few years later in *On the Road*, Kerouac mentioned whizzing through Indio on a bus heading back east, returning to his mother's house.

16. La Honda. For details about the sites in this area, please refer to *The Beat Generation in San Francisco*, pages 200–202.

17. Long Beach.

a. The visual artist better known as **Jess** was born in Long Beach on August 6, 1923, as Burgess Collins. His father, James Collins, worked as an engineer while the family was living at **119 Bay Shore Avenue.** During World War II, Jess worked on the Manhattan Project as a chemist, but in 1949 he enrolled in the California School of the Arts in San Francisco. It is interesting to note that some of his collages are inspired by chemical and alchemical themes. The following year Jess met Robert Duncan, and in 1951 he became his companion for the next thirty-seven years.

Joanne Kyger

Courtesy of the Allen Ginsberg Trust

b. **Joanne Kyger** spent some of her childhood in Long Beach. When she was five years old, her first published poem appeared in her school newspaper. Too young to write, she had to dictate the poem to her first grade teacher.

18. Los Angeles (see also specific cities within Los Angeles County, e.g., Long Beach, Venice, and so on).

a. In *On the Road* **Jack Kerouac's** character, Sal Paradise, frequently passed through **Hollywood**. On one occasion he describes arriving early in the morning when it was still gray, "like the dawn Joel McRea met Veronica Lake in the picture *Sullivan's Travels* in a diner." Kerouac tried to get a job in a drugstore at the corner of **Sunset and Vine** without any luck. Possibly it was the same Schwab's drugstore where Lana Turner was said to have been discovered. Then he tried the drive-in restaurants along **Hollywood Boulevard**, which he characterized as "a great screaming frenzy of cars." Eventually he gave up. On that trip Jack also stopped at the **Columbia Pictures Studio** at **1438 North Gower Street** to retrieve a rejected screenplay. Then, while waiting for his bus back to New York, he bought a loaf of bread and made ten salami sandwiches for the trip.

Years later, in 1956, Kerouac complained about the city in a letter to Gary Snyder. "But Los Angeles was a horror! First there was smog and my eyes hurt and burn; second, I got sinus and my nose leaded and hurt and head burned . . . ," Jack wrote as he waited for a train at the station. He even had time to compose a poem he titled "Little Main Street Blues: Los Angeles."

In November 1959, Kerouac returned to Hollywood yet again for the combined purposes of appearing on the Steve Allen Show and looking in on the production of *The Subterraneans* at the **Metro-Goldwyn-Mayer Studios** at **10202 West Washington Boulevard in Culver City**. At Steve Allen's expense he traveled in luxury via passenger train from the East Coast and stayed in California for ten days. With Steve Allen accompanying him on the piano, Jack read a beautiful passage from *Visions of Cody*. Since the producers wanted him to read from *On the Road*, he taped the sheet from *Cody* into the back

217

of the *Road* book, and no one ever knew the difference. Even though he was nervous and a bit drunk in front of the camera, it was a good performance at the pinnacle of his celebrity. Later Steve and Jack produced an entire album of words and music.

b. Hollywood once again hosted some of the Beats in 1978 during the filming of the movie *Heart Beat*. **Carolyn Cassady** consulted on the set at **Universal Studios, 110 Universal City Plaza**, as they made the movie version of her memoir of the same name. It featured Sissy Spacek (Carolyn), Nick Nolte (Neal) and John Heard (Kerouac). One day, after **William S. Burroughs** dropped by the

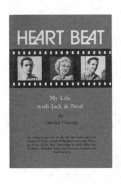

studio to see what was going on, he went to a dinner party given in his honor with guests Christopher Isherwood, Timothy Leary, Kenneth Tynan, Paul Getty Jr., and Tom Forcade, the publisher of *High Times* magazine. Burroughs stayed at the **Tropicana Motor Hotel** at **8585 Santa Monica Boulevard** in West Hollywood, where Tom Waits once lived in a back bungalow.

c. Although poet and archenemy of the Beats **Jack Spicer** was born in the Pasadena Hospital (technically a separate city) on January 30, 1925, he grew up in Los Angeles at **527 North Serrano Avenue**. His parents, John Lovely and Dorothy Clause Spicer, ran a small hotel there. When Jack was three years old, his mother became pregnant again and they sent Jack to Minnesota to live with his grandmother. Spicer never forgave his family for that. In 1943, after he graduated from **Fairfax High School** at **7850 Melrose Avenue**, he moved permanently to the San Francisco Bay Area and never spoke about his relatives again. Many of his friends even believed he was an orphan. Although he was an important member of the San Francisco Renaissance, he hated Beat writers with a passion. Spicer loathed the idea of the Beat Generation so much that he refused to allow Lawrence Ferlinghetti to sell his books at City Lights and published a nasty poem called "Ferlinghetti".

d. Although born on Staten Island, New York, in 1926, **Wallace Berman** moved with his family to **2836½ Hillcrest Drive** in Los Angeles in 1930 and lived and worked there for much of his life. Like Jack Spicer, Berman also attended **Fairfax High School**, but unlike Spicer, who managed to graduate, Berman was expelled for gambling. Between 1955 and 1964 Berman published nine issues of the avant-garde journal *Semina*. Included in the list of contributors are William S. Burroughs, Michael McClure, Allen Ginsberg, Philip Lamantia, and many other Beat writers. The unique creative community that grew up around Berman was recently documented in the beautiful book *Semina Culture: Wallace Berman and His Circle*. As an artist Berman exhibited in many local galleries including the **Ferus Gallery** at **736A North La Cienega Boulevard**. There his work created a furor and the gallery was shut down for showing "lewd material." In 1965 his small house at **10426 Crater Lane** in Beverly Glen was crushed by a mudslide. Although no one was hurt, the building where he had lived since 1953, containing all his artworks, was destroyed. Berman was devastated. In 1976 Berman was struck and killed near his home in Topanga Canyon by a drunk driver on the eve of his fiftieth birthday.

e. During the fall of 1962, **Diane Di Prima** visited Wallace Berman on Crater Lane for a few weeks and later that year moved to **Observation Drive** in the Topanga Canyon region with her new husband, Alan Marlowe. Another Topanga Canyon neighbor was artist **George Herms**.

f. Charles "Hank" Bukowski was born on August 16, 1920, in Andernach, Germany, but grew up in Los Angeles. As a child he lived at **4511 West 28th Street** and enrolled in the **Virginia Road Elementary School** in 1926. Later his family moved to a two-bedroom house at **2122 Longwood Avenue**, and while living there Bukowski suffered repeated beatings at the hands of his father. He graduated from **Los Angeles High School** in 1939, but that wasn't the end of the abuse. The following year his father threw all of Hank's possessions and manuscripts onto the front lawn and kicked him out of the house. Bukowski remained in the city for most of his life. In 2008 the Los Angeles City Council approved the designation of Bukowski's former bungalow at **5124 De Longpre Avenue**, where the writer lived from 1963 to 1972, as a cultural landmark.

g. Timothy Leary spent his last years in a small ranch house at **1016 Sunbrook**, overlooking Beverly Hills. Having decided to make his death an experience to be shared by everyone, he surrounded himself with friends and admirers. Thus, his death on May 31, 1996, was a continuation of his earlier idea to expand and chart the workings of the human mind. He kept in touch with the world until his final breath via a computer that had been installed in the small room behind the garage.

h. As a teenager, **David Meltzer** moved to Los Angeles in 1951. Three years later he began working in a junk store on **Santa Monica Boulevard**, and there he met artist Ed Kienholz, whose studio was nearby. Through Kienholz, Meltzer met Wally Berman and became a part of the Los Angeles arts community. He attended **Los Angeles City College** in 1955–56 and **UCLA** in 1956–57, before he moved permanently to San Francisco.

i. Shortly after his release from a New York prison, **Gregory Corso** came to Los Angeles looking for work in 1952. There he decided to try his hand at newspaper work. While he was living at the **Oxford Hotel** at **1120 Grand Avenue**, he landed a job with the *Los Angeles Examiner* at the corner of **Broadway and 11th Streets**. Corso was assigned to the newspaper's file morgue and was allowed to work one day a week as a cub reporter. This job lasted only a few months, but during that period Gregory met Boni Pedersen and fathered his first child, Sheri, a fact that he did not know about for many years. Nearly fifty years later, Sheri cared for Corso during his final illness, and he spent his last days at her home in Minnesota before his death in 2001.

j. One of the most often repeated stories about **Allen Ginsberg** is an incident that took place in Los Angeles on Halloween, October 31, 1956. Ginsberg and Gregory Corso had been invited by Lawrence Lipton to read in a private home as a benefit for the magazine *Coastlines*. In attendance that evening were about seventy people including the writer Anaïs Nin and poet Stuart Perkoff. When someone in the audience heckled Gregory, Allen came to his defense and challenged the heckler to "Take off your clothes and be naked." The man replied, "Take off your own clothes!" which prompted Allen to strip in front of the crowd. For some reason that silenced the heckler, and although Allen never did it again, the story was repeated as if it were something that Ginsberg did at every reading.

k. **John Cage** was born in Los Angeles on September 5, 1912. His parents were John Milton and Lucretia Harvey Cage. John's father was an inventor and his mother worked for the *Los Angeles Times*. As a fourth grader, Cage began to study the piano, and by the time he graduated from **Los Angeles High School** he was valedictorian of his class. Although he had originally hoped to become a writer, he became famous as one of the most innovative composers of the century. Cage championed the use of chance and nontraditional instruments in his work. He was a friend of many writers, including Allen Ginsberg, who influenced Cage's own writing and for whom Cage wrote a long poem titled "Writing Through Howl."

l. A major retrospective of the visual art work of **William S. Burroughs** was held at the **Los Angeles County Museum of Art** at **5905 Wilshire Boulevard** in July 1996. The show was called "Ports of Entry" and contained many of his remarkable paintings, collages, and assemblages. Of special interest were his paintings made by splattering paint-filled balloons with blasts from a shotgun.

m. Poet **Jack Hirschman** began teaching at **UCLA** in 1961. Living in nearby Venice, he became friends with many of the artists and writers who lived in Los Angeles including Wallace Berman and Stuart Perkoff. In 1966 Hirschman was fired from the university for his urging students to resist the draft during the Vietnam War. Hirschman's plan was to give everyone in his class an A grade so potential draftees could remain in school and maintain their student exemptions. The university alleged that his pacifist actions were "activities against the state." In 1973, after separating from his wife Ruth, Jack moved to San Francisco, where he became that city's fourth Poet Laureate in 2006.

n. **Hubert Selby Jr.**, best known for his book *Last Exit to Brooklyn*, died in the **Highland Park** district of Los Angeles on April 26, 2004, of lung disease. In 1967 Selby moved from Brooklyn to L.A. hoping to break his addiction to heroin. There he met his future wife but eventually wound up in the Los Angeles County Jail on possession charges. In prison he was finally able to kick his habit. He settled down with Suzanne to work as an adjunct professor in the **University of Southern California**'s writing program.

19. Los Gatos. For details about the sites in this area, please refer to *The Beat Generation in San Francisco,* pages 207–208.

20. Marin City. For details about the sites in this area, please refer to *The Beat Generation in San Francisco,* page 214.

21. Menlo Park. For details about the sites in this area, please refer to *The Beat Generation in San Francisco,* page 202.

22. Mill Valley. For details about the sites in this area, please refer to *The Beat Generation in San Francisco,* pages 214–216.

23. Millbrae. On April 10, 1953, **Neal Cassady** was injured in an accident on the Southern Pacific railroad tracks in Millbrae. As he was leaping from the train to set the brake on a boxcar, he stumbled and broke the bones in his ankle. He spent a month in the hospital and then months convalescing with his foot in a cast. That summer while Neal was recuperating from the accident, Allen Ginsberg lived with the Cassady family in San Jose.

24. Modesto. Poet and filmmaker **James Broughton** was born in Modesto on November 10, 1913. His wealthy family lived in a home at **1015 16th Street** where his father died during the influenza pandemic of 1919. It was in that house that Broughton had his first mystical vision at age three. He said that angels had sent a naked boy to him to foretell that he would become a poet.

25. Mojave. In *On the Road,* **Jack Kerouac** describes a car ride across the valley floor from Mojave up through the **Tehachapi Pass** with his Neal Cassady character, Dean,

Philip Lamantia, early 1980s

behind the wheel. On their way they flew past a women's prison and a cement factory before coasting down from the pass for the next thirty miles to save gas.

26. Mt. Shasta City. "**Philip Lamantia** loved Mt. Shasta for its extraordinary beauty and also for the strange cults that had developed there over the years," said Nancy Peters. During the 1970s and 1980s Lamantia often stayed in Mt. Shasta City, birdwatching and investigating paranormal phenomena reported in the area. Many people were said to have experienced strange flashes of light, apparitions, and unexplained visions. Some even reported meeting beings from the lost continent of Leumuria, all of which intrigued Lamantia and found their way into his poem "Shasta."

27. Mount Tamalpais. For details about the sites in this area, please refer to *The Beat Generation in San Francisco,* page 216.

28. Needles. Poet **Alice Notley**'s family moved to Needles from Bisbee, Arizona, when she was only two years old. She grew up in a house on **Erin Drive** while Notley's father ran the **Needles Auto Supply** at **419 Broadway**. Alice attended **Vista Colorado Elementary School** before graduating from **Needles Union**, the high school just up the hill from her house. It is no surprise that images of the desert feature prominently in several of her poems. Needles, on the Colorado River, is famous for its extreme heat. In New York, Alice married poet Ted Berrigan and became a prominent figure at the St. Mark's Poetry Project as a member of the Second Generation of the New York School.

29. Nevada City.

Gary Snyder bought wooded property in the Northern Sierras near here in 1966 and has lived in the mountains ever since. He and some Buddhist friends built a comfortable home which he called **Kitkitdizze** and constructed a zendo nearby for meditation. The forests and wildlife around his home always inspire his poetry. In 1974 Snyder won the Pulitzer Prize for his book, *Turtle Island.* The title refers to the ancient Native American name for America. In later years Snyder taught at the University of California in Davis and was inducted into the prestigious American Academy and Institute of Arts and Letters.

Gary Snyder

In the 1960s **Allen Ginsberg** bought the parcel of land next to Snyder's, where he and **Peter Orlovsky** built a small cabin they called **Bedrock Mortar**, after some distinctive rock formations. Allen's dream was to retire to the mountains in his old age, but that never worked out.

A few years before Ginsberg's death he sold his property to Snyder. For a while during the 1960s Gary and Allen toyed with the idea of inviting **Philip Whalen** and **Lew Welch** to live on the land as well. Later Lew Welch came to stay with Gary and it was from this spot, during a bout of depression, that Welch disappeared into the wilderness on May 23, 1971. He left a farewell note behind and took a revolver with him, but his body was never found.

30. Oakland.

a. **Robert Duncan** was born in Oakland on January 7, 1919, in a house at **1110 East 22nd Street** that was demolished long ago. According to the city directory, Robert Duncan's father, Edward Howard Duncan, was a "slinger" and lived here with his wife, Marguerite Wesley Duncan. Marguerite died shortly after Robert was born, another victim of the great influenza epidemic of that year. As was common at the time, his father put him up for adoption, and he was raised by the Symmes family in nearby Alameda. Duncan's earliest poems were published under the name of Robert Symmes, before he restored his original family name.

b. In 1961 **Andy Clausen** graduated from Oakland's **Bishop O'Dowd High School** at **9500 Stearns Avenue** and went on to study at six different colleges. Clausen was born André Laloux in Belgium in 1943, but was raised in Oakland. He is one of the most important poets of the newly christened "post-beat" school. Clausen was a particular favorite of Allen Ginsberg, who appeared onstage with him at many readings and who wrote the introduction for Clausen's *Without Doubt* in 1991.

c. Oakland was the focal point for many anti–Vietnam War demonstrations during the 1960s and 1970s. The **Oakland Army Induction Center**, once at **1515 Clay**, was the target of many of these protests. Blocking the entrance to "the gates of war" was the objective of the Merry Pranksters and Ken Kesey during their Berkeley rallies. One particular march was halted at the Oakland/Berkeley border, short of its goal. In October 1967 the demonstrators returned again, and Lawrence Ferlinghetti, Joan Baez, and Kay Boyle were arrested during their nonviolent protest. Later Gary Snyder, Richard Baker, and members of the San Francisco Zen Center came to the Oakland Army Terminal to protest the continuation of the war.

d. More than a decade before the Vietnam War, **Jack Kerouac** shipped out from the same **Army Terminal** docks on board the S.S. *William H. Carothers*. From Oakland the ship sailed through the Panama Canal, but once it arrived in New Orleans, Kerouac jumped ship. The story was retold in his book *Lonesome Traveler*.

e. The **Oakland Museum of California** at **1000 Oak Street** has an interesting exhibit on the Beats, which includes Henri Lenoir's superb collection of Beat memorabilia. For a while Lenoir owned the Vesuvio Bar in San Francisco, next door to the City Lights bookstore. During the Beatnik craze of the mid-fifties, Vesuvio's sold do-it-yourself Beatnik Kits to the tourists. One of these rare artifacts is on display in the museum. Items pertaining to Timothy Leary and Allen Ginsberg appear in a related exhibit on the 1960s counterculture.

f. **St. Augustine's Church** located at **400 Alcatraz Avenue**, is where William Everson received religious instruction following his conversion to Catholicism. On Christmas Eve 1948, Everson underwent an intense visionary experience and the following spring began formal studies here that led to his becoming a monk.

g. **St. Albert's College** is located at **5890 Birch Court**. In 1951, two years after William Everson converted to Catholicism, he entered the Dominican Order at this college. He adopted the name Brother Antoninus and remained a lay monk until 1969, when he left the order. During those years he published dozens of books of poetry, not always with the consent of his superiors.

31. Palo Alto. For details about the sites in this area, please refer to *The Beat Generation in San Francisco*, pages 202–205.

32. Paso Robles. In later years, Denver native **Haldon ("Hal") Chase** lived in **Rancho San Ignacio**, Paso Robles, where he built reproductions of harpsichords and ancient musical instruments. Chase became a friend of the Beats in 1944 when he was an undergraduate at Columbia University. A roommate of Ginsberg, Kerouac, and Burroughs, it was Chase who introduced them to a Denver friend by the name of Neal Cassady. After college Hal became a noted anthropologist associated with the Snake Blakeslee archaeological site and a specialist in Southwest archaeology.

Courtesy of the Allen Ginsberg Trust

Haldon Chase

33. Pixley. Immediately following his marriage to Carolyn Robinson on April 1, 1948, **Neal Cassady** went to work on the railroad in Pixley as a crew member of what he called "the potato local." The town in the Southern Central Valley was so small that Carolyn couldn't even find it on the map. Neal worked from nine a.m. to seven p.m. and slept in an old Pullman car on a siding. Isolated, he did not have much time for anything except eating, sleeping, reading, and working.

34. Rancho Palos Verdes. Later in his life, **Charles**

Bukowski earned enough money to buy a home in Rancho Palos Verdes, a quiet, affluent suburb of L.A. His house was not far from the **Green Hills Memorial Park** at **27501 South Western Avenue**, where Bukowski was buried following his death on March 9, 1994. His epitaph is short and summed up his philosphy: "Don't Try."

35. Sacramento. Poet **William Everson** was born in Sacramento on September 12, 1912. Shortly after his birth his family moved to the small agricultural town of Selma in California's Central Valley. As a conscientious objector during World War II, Everson served in the Civilian Public Service in Waldport, Oregon and in Weaverville, California, before taking the robes of a monk in the Dominican Order as Brother Antoninus.

36. San Bruno. For details about the sites in this area, please refer to *The Beat Generation in San Francisco,* pages 199–200.

37. San Francisco. In this city are some of the most important sites related to the Beat Generation in California. For details about those sites, please refer to *The Beat Generation in San Francisco.* As a frame of reference, five of the key points of interest are listed below.

    a. City Lights Bookstore, 261 Columbus Avenue
    b. Cassady's house, 29 Russell Street
    c. Ginsberg's apartment, 1010 Montgomery
    d. Ferlinghetti's apartment, 339 Chestnut
    e. Six Gallery, 3119 Fillmore

39. San Jose. **Neal and Carolyn Cassady** made their home at **1047 East Santa Clara Street** in San Jose from 1952 to 1954. For this and other details about the sites in this area, please refer to *The Beat Generation in San Francisco,* pages 205–206.

40. San Luis Obispo.

a. Early in 1953, **Jack Kerouac** decided to distance himself from New York, in part to avoid the legal suit asking for child support that had been launched by his second wife, Joan Haverty. When the Southern Pacific offered him work as a brakeman, he seized the opportunity to head for California. At the same time Neal Cassady was recovering from a seriously broken ankle, but instead of moving in with Neal and Carolyn in San Jose, Jack found a cheap room at the **Colonial Hotel**, then at **103 Santa Barbara Avenue** in San Luis Obispo. Kerouac wrote to his mother to tell her that he would soon have enough money to bring her out to join him. They'd buy a trailer to live in for a year or so, "right on the sea," he said. But by May, Kerouac had grown tired of the drudgery of a full-time job and quit the railroad, signing on to a ship bound for New York.

b. On September 12, 1970, **Timothy Leary** escaped from a minimum-security prison, part of the **California Men's Colony** at San Luis Obispo, where he was held on drug-related charges. It was a dramatic escape that involved

Courtesy of the Allen Ginsberg Trust

Timothy Leary and Neal Cassady on the Merry Prankster's bus

Leary's climbing along a cable high over the prison fence. Since May of that year he had been serving a twenty-year sentence and regarded himself as a political prisoner. From California he fled to Algeria with the help of the Weather Underground, and there he hid out with Eldridge Cleaver and the Black Panthers.

41. San Mateo. For details about the sites in this area, please refer to *The Beat Generation in San Francisco,* page 200.

42. San Quentin. For details about the sites in this area, please refer to *The Beat Generation in San Francisco,* page 217.

43. San Rafael. Writer and Kerouac scholar **John Montgomery** died of a heart attack on June 5, 1992, in the **Kaiser Hospital** in San Rafael. Montgomery had been the model for Kerouac's characters Henry Morley in *The Dharma Bums* and Alex Fairbrother in *Desolation Angels.* His frequent treks with Kerouac and Snyder into the Sierra Mountains featured prominently in those books.

44. Santa Barbara.
a. Poet **Joanne Kyger** went to high school in Santa Barbara, just one of the many towns she lived in as the daughter of a career naval officer. At the **University of California, Santa Barbara** she was a philosophy major, but she left school in 1957 one unit shy of a degree. While living here she joined a poetry workshop held at the **Santa Barbara Public Library** at **40 East Anapamu Street**.
b. **Kenneth Rexroth** spent his final years in Santa Barbara. After accepting a teaching position at the **University of California, Santa Barbara** in the fall of 1968, Rexroth moved away from San Francisco permanently. He took

up residence at the **Dower House** on **East Pepper Lane** in Mendocito, a beautiful three-acre property. There he filled the house with his enormous collection of books and artworks. He died in that house on June 6, 1982. Rexroth's body was interred on the grounds of the **Santa Barbara Cemetery Association** on a hilltop overlooking the ocean. His epitaph quotes one of his own poems: "As the full moon rises / The swan sings / In sleep / On the lake of the mind."

45. Santa Cruz. For details about the sites in this area, please refer to *The Beat Generation in San Francisco*, page 209.

46. Santa Monica.

a. Neeli Cherkovski was born in Santa Monica on July 1, 1945. He grew up as Neeli Cherry in San Bernardino, the son of Sam and Claire Cherry, bookshop owners and through his parents inherited a love of books. He received his B.A. from **California State University** in Los Angeles. A longtime friend of Los Angeles writer Charles Bukowski, Cherkovski wrote a wonderful biography of him titled *Hank*. Later, Neeli moved to San Francisco and became a well-known and prolific poet himself. He wrote the first full-length biography of Lawrence Ferlinghetti, *Ferlinghetti: A Biography* in 1979.

b. The Fugs, an irreverent rock group organized by poets Ed Sanders and Tuli Kupferberg, performed in Santa Monica in 1967 at the height of their underground popularity. Sanders had made the cover of *Life* magazine that February, but The Fugs' inflammatory lyrics were too radical for even the most progressive record labels and radio stations. Allen Ginsberg was also in town at the time to take part in a sold-out benefit to raise money to defend Sanders against obscenity charges stemming from his publication of *Fuck You: A Magazine of the Arts*.

Photograph by Elsa Dorfman

The Music Lesson: Ginsberg & Dylan on the Rolling Thunder Revue. Dylan

Bob Dylan and Allen Ginsberg

c. Allen Ginsberg returned to Santa Monica many times in his later years to perform at **McCabe's Guitar Shop**, still located on **Pico Boulevard**. Often while in Los Angeles, Ginsberg visited his friend Bob Dylan, and occasionally they recorded together in Dylan's sound studio. Here they worked on the final editing of *Renaldo and Clara*, the movie Dylan made during his Rolling Thunder tour.

47. Sausalito. For details about the sites in this area, please refer to *The Beat Generation in San Francisco*, pages 213–214.

48. Selma.

a. Born in Sacramento, poet **William Everson** grew up in the farming town of Selma, where he was raised as a Christian Scientist by his mother. He graduated from **Selma High School** at **3125 Wright Street** and then went on to Fresno State College in 1931, long before his conversion to Catholicism.

b. **Jack Kerouac** spent time in Selma with his Mexican girlfriend, Bea Franco, a period he described in *On the Road*. One day a stoned Jack and Bea "roamed the quiet leafy square of the little California town—a whistle stop on the S.P." Stretched out on his back in the middle of the lawn, Jack recited a scene from the movie *Of Mice and Men* from memory. About five miles out of town, he and Bea found jobs as seasonal workers picking grapes. To Jack it was a short-lived adventure, but to Bea, this hard work was the only life she knew.

49. Tassajara Springs. In the hills above Big Sur at **39171 Tassajara Road**, Carmel Valley, sits Tassajara Springs, a Buddhist training center. Gary Snyder, Alan Watts, and others gave benefit readings to help the Zen Center purchase property here. In 1975 poet Philip Whalen was put in charge of the Zen Mountain Center. Whalen first came to Tassajara in 1972 for a training period and was ordained a Zen priest at Tassajara in 1973 before he became the *shuso* (head monk) two years

Philip Whalen (in robes) with friends

later. Many of his poems were inspired by his life here. Another frequent Buddhist visitor to Tassajara was poet Diane Di Prima.

50. Trinity Alps Wilderness. After suffering a breakdown exacerbated by heavy drinking, poet **Lew Welch** found refuge in an abandoned cabin in the mountains near Forks of Salmon for more than a year. The cabin had been built by an ex-Wobblie in an extremely remote area known as Rat Flat, but soon Welch moved to another old cabin closer to town and the post office. Lew wrote *Hermit Poems* and "The Way Back" series here between 1962 and January 1964, and supported himself by taking on occasional work with the Forest Service.

51. Tulare. On one of their *On the Road* trips, **Neal Cassady** and **Jack Kerouac** picked up a hitchhiker named Alfred. He told them that although he had no money with him, once they got to Tulare, he could get some from his aunt who ran a grocery store in town. Once they arrived in Tulare, though, there was no money. It turned out that before their arrival Alfred's aunt had shot her husband and been sent to jail.

52. Tuolumne. Lord Buckley, originally named Richard Myrle Buckley, was born in Tuolumne on April 5, 1906, into a large family. Richard's father, William, worked in the gold mines that dot the region. During the 1950s, the satiric monologues delivered by Lord Buckley became popular with hip audiences across the country. His routines combined the hipster language of jazz musicians with regional dialects, and a little British aristocracy thrown into make an amusing amalgam. Like Lenny Bruce he struggled continually with the censors. He died in New York City in 1960.

Courtesy of Joanne Kyger

Joanne Kyger

53. Vallejo. On November 19, 1934, **Joanne Kyger** was born northwest of San Francisco in a hospital in Vallejo. Her parents, J. Holmes and Anne Lamont Kyger, moved around continually for her father's naval assignments. After Vallejo they lived in China, Pensacola, Long Beach, Lake Bluff, Illinois, Upper Darby, Pennsylvania, and finally Santa Barbara, where Joanne lived long enough to attend both high school and college.

54. Venice.

a. Poet **Stuart Perkoff** moved to Venice in 1952 and lived there on and off until his death from cancer on June 24, 1974. During those years, Venice West, as it was called, was the bohemian center of Southern California. In 1956 Perkoff's first book, *The Suicide Room,* was published by Jonathan Williams's press, Jargon Books. Addicted to drugs, Perkoff served several years in prison for dealing and drifted around the country after his release. He co-founded the **Venice West Cafe** at **7 Dudley Avenue**, which became the central gathering place for avant-garde artists and poets until it was forced to close in 1966.

b. Venice was immortalized by **Lawrence Lipton** in *The Holy Barbarians*, a 1959 sociological study of the Beat community. Lipton was highly influential in the poetry and jazz movement that became popular here in the late 1950s. He died on July 9, 1975, at his home in Venice.

The national news media often focused on the "Beatnik" lifestyle of the Venice Beats at the expense of the more serious San Francisco and New York Beat writers. The cover blurb for *The Holy Barbarians* says it all: "At last the complete story of the 'Beats'—that hip, cool, frantic generation of new Bohemians who are turning the American scale of values inside out."

c. Other writers associated with the Beat Generation have also lived in Venice. **Philip Whalen** stayed with a friend there in 1951 while he worked in the North American Aircraft factory, now part of Rockwell International. **Jack Hirschman** lived in Venice from 1967 to 1971 while teaching at **UCLA**. He had a small place on **Quarterdeck Street** on the marina peninsula.

55. Watsonville. For details about the sites in this area, please refer to *The Beat Generation in San Francisco*, page 209.

56. Woodfords. This Sierra town is just south of Lake Tahoe, very close to the Nevada border. In 1953, **Philip Lamantia** participated in Washo Indian peyote rites in nearby Diamond Valley. It was a profound experience for the poet and precipitated his interest in native cultures of Mexico and the United States All of this is reflected in his poetry.

57. Woodland. Artist **George Herms** was born in the small farm town of Woodland in 1935 and took up art in the 1950s without having any formal training. For most of his career, Herms remained on the fringe of the art world, showing his quirky work wherever he could. His assemblages and collage works were finally exhibited to a nationwide audience in 1995 during the Whitney Museum's show "Beat Culture and the New America: 1950–1965."

58. Yosemite.

Yosemite National Park has figured in the lives and writings of several Beat authors. In 1955 **Gary Snyder** worked as a trail crewman in Yosemite. After being blacklisted by the Forest Service in Washington state for being a member of what the government considered to be a "communist" labor union, Snyder found work in Yosemite only because they failed to check his background before they hired him.

That same summer, **Allen Ginsberg** and **Peter Orlovsky** made a camping trip to Yosemite from San Francisco in their car, which they had nicknamed "the hearse." From there Orlovsky hitchhiked back to New York and Ginsberg returned to San Francisco where he began to write "Howl," his most famous poem.

ALASKA

1. Arctic Ocean. In 1956 **Allen Ginsberg** found work as a yeoman on a freighter that supplied the DEW (Distant Early Warning) Line along the northern coast

Courtesy of the Allen Ginsberg Trust

Allen Ginsberg in Merchant Marine hat

of Alaska. On July 27 he passed through the Bering Straight and anchored off **Icy Cape**. In memory of Naomi, his Russian-born mother, who had died a few weeks earlier, he tossed some coins from the deck as his ship, the USNS *Sgt. Jack J. Pendleton*, passed within a few miles of Russia's coast. "Ice and the death of my mother—I wonder if I can see God in the white floes and brilliant black light," he wrote in a letter. While anchored offshore, Ginsberg used the ship's mimeo machine to print fifty-two copies of a poem titled *Siesta in Xbalba,* his first published pamphlet. The ship's crew was not allowed on shore for fear of spreading measles to the native population, so Ginsberg never set foot on land.

Gary Snyder had better luck in 1979 when he visited **Point Barrow** in the dead of winter with his second wife, Masa. While visiting **Anchorage** on that same trip, Gary read poetry from *Turtle Island* while Masa did some Indian dances in front of an audience at **Alaska Pacific University's Grant Hall** at **4101 University Drive**.

2. Dillingham. Over the years this tiny town has hosted several authors with links to the Beat Generation. In 1983, **Ken Kesey** visited Dillingham with his son Jed to research *Sailor Song,* a fictional story based in Alaska. It was to be the last trip they took together, as Jed was tragically killed the following year in a highway accident. About that same time, **Gary Snyder** also came to town and wrote the poem "Dillingham, Alaska, The Willow Tree Bar," immortalizing a workingman's saloon that is still in business. The poem begins: "Drills chatter full of mud and compressed air / all across the globe, / low-ceilinged bars, we hear the same new songs. . . ." Snyder traveled throughout Alaska for a month, visiting remote communities to make recommendations to the Alaska Humanities Forum for future programs and conferences. In 1985, Gary returned to the **Brooks Range** in northern Alaska to teach an experimental field course on wilderness philosophy.

3. Haines. Near Haines, which was once a supply center for the Yukon Gold Rush, **Gary Snyder** was joined by Nanao Sakaki and Ron and Suzie Scollon. Together they took the strenuous hike to the top of nearby **Mt. Ripinsky**, a few miles out of town. In 1986 the Scollons founded the **Axe Handle Academy**, a progressive school that they named in honor of Snyder's book of poems, *Axe Handles*.

4. Skagway. In 1982 **Ken Kesey** visited Skagway to help write the ending for the film *Never Cry Wolf*, which was being shot on location by director Carroll Ballard. Kesey was attracted by the rugged beauty and energy he found in Alaska. Inspired by the area, Ken created a fictional Alaskan village, which he called Kuinak, as the locale of his next book, *Sailor Song*. The story, which takes place thirty years in the future, is set in a town overrun by filmmakers who are shooting a children's movie. The central love affair in the book plays out as man's existence on earth comes to an end.

HAWAII

1. O'Ahu. Honolulu.

a. In 1957 the freighter S.S. *Sappa Creek* docked in Honolulu for a few days. **Gary Snyder** was aboard, working as a seaman to earn money for his studies at a Buddhist monastery in Japan. On that voyage Snyder traveled around the world before returning to Kyoto. Honolulu was also the home of **Robert Aitken Roshi**, whose Diamond Sangha at **2747 Waiomao Road** became the spiritual model for Gary Snyder's meditation group at Kitkitdizze, Gary's home in the Sierra mountains. Aitken Roshi visited Snyder's Ring of Bone Zendo in California many times and led sesshins there each August.

b. From 1964 until 1972, scientist and naturalist **Gregory Bateson** served as the director of the Oceanic Institute, part of the **Hawai'i Pacific University** at **1164 Bishop Street**. In the late 1950s, it was Bateson who had offered to give Allen Ginsberg his first LSD as part of a research project at Stanford, an experiment that was to change Ginsberg's life.

c. In March 1972, on their way to a reading tour in Australia, **Allen Ginsberg, Lawrence Ferlinghetti** and his son, **Lorenzo**, stopped in O'Ahu to visit a friend of Allen's who was a botanist and an expert in psychedelics.

d. In October 1977, **Allen Ginsberg** returned to Hawaii to attend the East-West Convergence Conference. Ginsberg delivered a talk comparing Himalayan-American *Vajrayana* practice with the LSD experience. While on the islands Allen did all the usual tourist things, including visiting the island of Kauai and the Kalalau Valley, where a remake of the movie *King Kong* had recently been filmed. In Hawaii Ginsberg wrote several poems including "What's Dead?" and "Slack Key Guitar Blues."

2. Maui. Michael McClure once stayed in a little hermitage in the rain forest on Maui next to a Tibetan Buddhist *stupa*. The windows in his room were shaped like crescent moons and stars. There, as elsewhere, McClure was inspired by the beauty of the natural world.

ACKNOWLEDGMENTS

While putting this book together, I crossed the country several times looking for elusive "Beat" sites. Countless people along the way helped and guided me to my destinations. First and foremost, Nancy Peters steered me through the initial stages in the creation of this manual. She suggested several important locations and features that eventually found their way into the pages that follow. Garrett Caples, my editor at City Lights, meticulously led me through version after version, always with an eye on making the book as accurate and readable as possible. Elaine Katzenberger, publisher of City Lights books, who early on saw the importance of documenting the grassroots nature of the Beat Generation, has earned my heartfelt appreciation as well.

Other people helped me on my journey and answered what must have seemed like never-ending questions. Among those guides, I'd like to especially thank:

Carolyn Cassady, Ann Charters, Neeli Cherkovski, Robert Creeley, Amy Evans, Lawrence Ferlinghetti, Bill Gargan, Allen Ginsberg, Peter Hale, Joyce Johnson, Rob Johnson, Brenda Knight, David Kruh, Joanna McClure, Kaye McDonough, Michael McClure, Tim Moran, Colleen Nickerson (Waldport Heritage Museum), Alice Notley, Bob Rosenthal, John Sampas, Ed Sanders, Sally Schubert, Gary Snyder, and Tony Trigilio.

The photographs in this book were made available through the courtesy of many people. In particular I'd like to thank the Allen Ginsberg Trust for access to Allen's enormous archive at Stanford University. Gordon Ball, Carolyn Cassady, Robert Cohen, Elsa Dorfman, Derek Fenner, Bill Gargan, Cassidy Hughes, Larry Keenan, Joanne Kyger, Helen MacLeod, Tim Moran, Hank O'Neal, Ron Padgett, Nancy Peters, Bob Rosenthal, Ettore Sottsass, and John Suiter have generously allowed their photographs to be reproduced.

And finally I am indebted to my wife Judy, who took to the road alongside me, tracking down the ghosts of the Beats wherever we could find them. Without her help and support, none of this would have been possible.

Pages 43, 159: Photographs courtesy of Ron Padgett.

Page 47: Photograph by Bill Gargan. Copyright © Bill Gargan.

Page 60: Photograph by Bob Rosenthal. Copyright © Bob Rosenthal.

Page 89: Photograph by Timothy Moran. Copyright © Timothy Moran.

Page 91 (top and bottom): Photographs by Cassidy Hughes. Copyright © Cassidy Hughes.

Page 102: Photograph by Betty Schneider. Courtesy the Estate of Lee Streiff.

Page 110: Photograph by Larry Keenan. Copyright © Larry Keenan. Courtesy Larry Keenan.

Page 126: Photograph by Ettore Sottsass. Copyright © Ettore Sottsass.

Pages 154 (bottom), 155: Photograph by R.I. Sutherland-Cohen. Copyright © R.I. Sutherland-Cohen.

Pages 190, 224: Photographs by Nancy Joyce Peters. Copyright © Nancy Joyce Peters.

Page 207: Photograph by John Suiter. Copyright © John Suiter.

Page 236: Photograph courtesy of Joanne Kyger.

BIBLIOGRAPHY OF BOOKS CITED

Allen, Donald. *The New American Poetry 1945-1960*. NY: Grove, 1960.

Antler. *Factory*. SF: City Lights, 1980.

Bremser, Bonnie. *Troia: Mexican Memoirs*. NY: Croton Press, 1969.

Bremser, Ray. *Poems Of Madness*. NY: Paperback Gallery, 1965.

Brooks, Eugene. *Rites of Passage*. Privately printed, 1973.

Brossard, Chandler. *Who Walk In Darkness*. NY: New Directions, 1952.

Burroughs, William S. *Cobble Stone Gardens*. Cherry Valley, NY: Cherry Valley Editions, 1976.

Burroughs, William S. *Junkie*. NY: Ace, 1953.

Burroughs, William S. *Junky*. NY: Penguin, 1977.

Burroughs, William S. *The Naked Lunch*. Paris: Olympia, 1959.

Burroughs, William S. *Queer*. NY: Viking Penguin, 1985.

Burroughs, William S. *The Retreat Diaries*. NY: City Moon, 1976.

Burroughs, William S. and Jack Kerouac. *And the Hippos Were Boiled in Their Tanks*. NY: Grove, 2008.

Burroughs, William Jr. *Kentucky Ham*. NY: Dutton, 1973.

Burroughs, William Jr. *Speed*. NY: Olympia, 1970.

Capote, Truman. *In Cold Blood*. NY: Random House, 1965.

Cassady, Carolyn. *Heart Beat*. Berkeley, CA: Creative Arts, 1976.

Cassady, Neal. *The First Third*. SF: City Lights, 1971.

Cherkovski, Neeli. *Ferlinghetti: A Biography*. Garden City, NY: Doubleday, 1979.

Clausen, Andy. *Without Doubt*. Oakland, CA: Zeitgeist, 1991.

Corso, Gregory. *The Vestal Lady on Brattle And Other Poems*. Cambridge, MA: Richard Brukenfeld, 1955.

Creeley, Robert. *All That Is Lovely in Men*. Asheville, NC: Jonathan Williams, 1955.

De Loach, Allen. *The East Side Scene: American Poetry, 1960–1965*. Buffalo, NY: SUNY Buffalo, 1968.

Dorn, Edward. *The Newly Fallen*. NY: Totem, 1961.

Duncan, Michael. *Semina Culture: Wallace Berman and His Circle*. NY: Distributed Art, 2005.

Ferlinghetti, Lawrence. *Mule Mountain Dreams*. Bisbee, AZ: Bisbee Press Collective and Cochise Fine Arts, 1980.

Ferlinghetti, Lawrence. *The Sea and Ourselves at Cape Ann*. Madison, WI: Red Ozier, 1979.

Gaddis, William. *The Recognitions*. NY: Harcourt, Brace and Co., 1955.

Genet, Jean. *May Day Speech*. SF: City Lights, 1970.

Ginsberg, Allen. *The Book of Martyrdom and Artifice*. NY: DaCapo Press, 2006.

Ginsberg, Allen. *Howl and Other Poems.* SF: City Lights, 1956.

Ginsberg, Allen. *Kaddish and Other Poems.* SF: City Lights, 1961.

Ginsberg, Allen. *Siesta in Xbalba.* Privately printed, 1956.

Ginsberg, Allen and Kenneth Koch. *Making It Up.* NY: Catchword Papers, 1979.

Ginsberg, Louis. *The Everlasting Minute and Other Lyrics.* NY: Liveright, 1937.

Harrington, Alan. *The Secret Swinger.* NY: Knopf, 1966.

Haverty Kerouac, Joan. *Nobody's Wife: The Smart Aleck and the King of Beats.* Creative Arts, 2000.

Holmes, John Clellon. *Go.* NY: Scribner's, 1952.

Holmes, John Clellon. *The Horn.* NY: Random House, 1958.

Holmes, John Clellon. *Visitor: Jack Kerouac in Old Saybrook.* California, PA: Unspeakable Visions of the Individual, 1980.

Huncke, Herbert. *The Herbert Huncke Reader.* NY: William Morrow, 1997.

Johnson, Joyce. *Minor Characters.* Boston: Houghton Mifflin, 1983.

Johnson, Rob. *The Lost Years of William S. Burroughs.* College Station, TX: Texas A&M University Press, 2006.

Jones, Hettie. *How I Became Hettie Jones.* NY: Dutton, 1990.

Kerouac, Jack. *Atop an Underwood: Early Stories and Other Writings.* NY: Viking, 1999.

Kerouac, Jack. *Big Sur.* NY: Farrar, Straus and Cudahy, 1962.

Kerouac, Jack. *Desolation Angels.* NY: Coward-McCann, 1965.

Kerouac, Jack. *The Dharma Bums.* NY: Viking, 1958.

Kerouac, Jack. *Doctor Sax.* NY: Grove, 1959.

Kerouac, Jack. *Lonesome Traveler.* NY: McGraw-Hill, 1960.

Kerouac, Jack. *Maggie Cassidy.* NY: Avon, 1959.

Kerouac, Jack. *Mexico City Blues.* NY: Grove, 1959.

Kerouac, Jack. *On the Road.* NY: Viking, 1957.

Kerouac, Jack. *Pic.* NY: Grove, 1971.

Kerouac, Jack. *Satori in Paris.* NY: Grove, 1966.

Kerouac, Jack. *The Subterraneans.* NY: Grove, 1958.

Kerouac, [Jack] John. *The Town and the City.* NY: Harcourt, Brace and Co., 1950.

Kerouac, Jack. *Vanity of Duluoz.* NY: Coward-McCann, 1968.

Kerouac, Jack. *Visions of Cody.* NY: McGraw-Hill, 1973.

Kerouac, Jack. *Visions of Gerard.* NY: Farrar, Straus and Co., 1963.

Kerouac, Jack, Albert Saijo and Lew Welch. *Trip Trap.* Bolinas, CA: Grey Fox, 1973.

Kerouac, Jan. *Baby Driver.* NY: St. Martin's, 1981.

Kerouac-Parker, Edie. *You'll Be Okay: My Life With Jack Kerouac.* SF: City Lights, 2007.

Kesey, Ken. *One Flew Over the Cuckoo's Nest.* NY: Viking, 1962.

Kesey, Ken. *Sailor Song.* NY: Viking, 1992.

Kesey, Ken. *Sometimes a Great Notion.* NY: Viking, 1964.

Kinsey, Alfred. *Sexual Behavior in the Human Male.* Philadelphia: W.B. Saunders, 1948.

Lamantia, Philip. *Blood of the Air.* SF: Four Seasons Foundation, 1970.

Lamantia, Philip. *Meadowlark West.* SF: City Lights, 1986.

Landesman, Jay. *Rebel Without Applause.* NY: Paragon House, 1987.

Lee, Harper. *To Kill a Mockingbird.* Philadelphia: Lippincott, 1960.

Lipton, Lawrence. *The Holy Barbarians.* NY: Julian Messner, 1959.

McClure, Joanna. *Wolf Eyes.* SF: Bearthm, 1974.

Mailer, Norman. *The White Negro.* SF: City Lights, 1960.

Micheline, Jack. *River Of Red Wine.* Privately printed, 1958.

Miller, Henry. *Tropic Of Cancer.* Paris: Obelisk, 1934.

Montgomery, John. *Kerouac At the Wild Boar And Other Skirmishes.* San Anselmo, CA: Fels & Firn, 1986.

Montgomery, John. *Kerouac We Knew.* San Anselmo, CA: Fels & Firn, 1987.

Morgan, Bill. *The Beat Generation In New York: A Walking Tour of Jack Kerouac's City.* SF: City Lights, 1997.

Morgan, Bill. *The Beat Generation In San Francisco: A Literary Tour.* SF: City Lights, 2003.

Morgan, Ted. *Literary Outlaw: The Life and Times of William S. Burroughs.* NY: Henry Holt, 1988.

O'Hara, Frank. *Lunch Poems.* SF: City Lights, 1964.

Olson, Charles. *Call Me Ishmael: A Study Of Melville.* NY: Reynal and Hitchcock, 1947.

Olson, Charles. *The Maximus Poems.* NY: Jargon/Corinth, 1960.

Padgett, Ron. *Oklahoma Tough: My Father, King Of the Tulsa Bootleggers.* Norman, OK: University of Oklahoma Press, 2003.

Padgett, Ron. *Tulsa Kid.* Z Press, 1979.

Patchen, Kenneth. *Fables and Other Little Tales.* Highlands, NC: Jonathan Williams, 1953.

Patchen, Kenneth. *Poems Of Humor & Protest.* SF: City Lights, 1956.

Perkoff, Stuart. *The Suicide Room.* Karlsruhe, West Germany: Jonathan Williams, 1956.

Pommy-Vega, Janine. *Poems To Fernando.* SF: City Lights, 1968.

Ray, Tom. *Yellowstone Red.* Philadelphia: Dorrance, 1948.

Sanders, Ed. *Poem From Jail.* SF: City Lights, 1963.

Selby, Hubert. *Last Exit To Brooklyn.* NY: Grove, 1964.

Snyder, Gary. *Axe Handles: Poems.* SF: North Point, 1983.

Snyder, Gary. *Turtle Island.* NY: New Directions, 1974.

Southern, Terry. *Flash and Filigree.* NY: Coward-McCann, 1958.

Southern, Terry. *Red Dirt Marijuana.* NY: New American Library, 1967.

Suzuki, D.T. *Essays in Zen Buddhism: First Series.* London: Luzac and Co., 1927.

Talayesva, Don. *Sun Chief: The Autobiography Of a Hopi Indian.* New Haven, CT: Yale University Press, 1942.

Thompson, Hunter. *Hell's Angels.* NY: Random House, 1967.

Wieners, John. *Pressed Wafer.* Buffalo: Upstairs Gallery Press, 1967.

Williams, William Carlos. *Paterson.* NY: New Directions, 1946-58.

Williams, William Carlos. *Pictures From Breughel And Other Poems.* NY: New Directions, 1962.

Wolfe, Thomas. *Look Homeward, Angel.* NY: Scribner's, 1929.

INDEX

The Beat Generation in New York

A Walking Tour of Jack Kerouac's City

Edited by Bill Morgan

Set off on the errant trail of the Beat experience in the city that inspired many of Jack Kerouac's best-loved novels including *On the Road, Vanity of Duluoz, The Town and the City*, and *Desolation Angels*. This is the ultimate guide to Kerouac's New York, packed with photos of the Beat Generation, and filled with undercover information and little-known anecdotes.

The Beat Generation in San Francisco

A Literary Tour

Edited by Bill Morgan

The ultimate literary guide to San Francisco, packed with fabulous photos and anecdotes.

A blow-by-blow unearthing of the places where the Beat writers first came to full bloom: the rooms where Ginsberg wrote "Howl," site of the Six Gallery reading, Gary Snyder's zen cottage, the ghostly railroad yards where Kerouac and Cassady worked, and much more!